Seeds

Some Good Ways to Improve Our Schools

by
Cynthia Parsons

Woodbridge Press / Santa Barbara, California

Published and distributed by

Woodbridge Press Publishing Company
Post Office Box 6189
Santa Barbara, California 93160

Copyright © 1985 by Cynthia Parsons

Distributed simultaneously in the United States and Canada.

Printed in the United States of America.

Library of Congress Cataloging in Publication Data.

Parsons, Cynthia.
  Seeds : some good ways to improve our schools.

  Includes index.
    1. Education—United States—Aims and objectives.
  2. Public schools—United States.   I. Title.
  LA217.P37   1985   370'.973   84-29160
  ISBN 0-88007-148-6

Dedication

For four master teachers:
Adèle, Betty,
Edie, Milton.

Contents

About the Author   9

Preface   11

Chapter One   Improving the Ethos   14
   Introduction: Harold Howe II

Chapter Two   Improving Teachers   46
   Introduction: Mary Hatwood Futrell

Chapter Three   Improving Principals   83

Chapter Four   Improving Discipline   115
   Introduction: Schuyler M. Meyer, Jr.

Chapter Five   Improving the Curriculum   139
   Introduction: A. Graham Down

Chapter Six   Improving the Budget   178

Chapter Seven   Improving Parents   194
   Introduction: Mildred E. Jones

Checklist Index   215

About the Author

Cynthia Parsons started her teaching career (1948) tutoring two children (using the Calvert system) on an island off the coast of Savannah, Georgia. Next she taught at a private school in the mountains of Southern California (Desert Sun, renamed Elliott Pope Preparatory School) and watched over nine children (ages three through nine) in a four-room dormitory.

She taught under Grace Fernald in the UCLA Clinic School the summer of 1950, working with children with learning disabilities. Wanting to learn how to write, she left the classroom for *The Christian Science Monitor* newsroom as a "copy boy." And followed that by operating a small private experimental school on the West bank of the Connecticut River in Putney, Vermont.

On then to North Adams and Westwood, Massachusetts; to Greenwich, Connecticut; and to Tarrytown, New York, teaching in their public schools and eventually (late '50s) becoming deeply committed to new math and the Madison Project then headquartered at Syracuse University.

In 1962, she joined *The Christian Science Monitor* as its education editor, serving there some 14 years (1962–1969 and 1974–1982). For three years (1970–1973), she was a senior program officer in the National Institute of Education's Experimental Schools Program; and for one year (1969–1970), education editor at the World Bank (International Bank for Reconstruction and Development). Her first book on school reform, *Schools Can Change*, was published in 1969.

Her home is a one-room white frame schoolhouse (circa 1874) located in Gassetts, Vermont. Since leaving the *Monitor* in 1982, she has been a visiting scholar at Geelong College in Geelong, Australia, and at Robert College in Istanbul, Turkey; also a visiting instructor at both Dartmouth and the University of Vermont.

9

Preface

I've visited scores of marvelous schools (even taught in a couple), watched hundreds of master teachers create magic, applauded brilliant administrators, hugged (and been hugged by) children unable to contain their joy from learning something compellingly interesting.

That's why I've spent the past year and a half writing SEEDS.

At first I was going to call this book, "180 Ways To Improve Schools," but discovered I was just about the only one who knew that the majority of states were required to keep public schools open for precisely that many days. Then I was going to call it simply, "Some Ways To Improve Schools." Next: "Some Ways To Improve Our Schools"; and finally, "Some Good Ways To Improve Our Schools."

But my youngest brother, Sherm Clark, an engineering type, flipping through an early draft of the first three chapters, snorted and said, "What you have here is a farrago of horses and rabbits!"

Some of the ideas were (and still are) huge—would require dramatic changes in public schools and schooling. Some were smaller—either in their intended effect or in the effort needed to implement them.

I thought long and hard, though, about those horses and rabbits. Perhaps you know about the French cook who was challenged by a customer while eating her specialty—Rabbit Stew. Seems he thought he detected some horsemeat. Madame Flambé readily admitted to making her rabbit stew half and half, horse and rabbit; one horse and one rabbit.

After all, this was my little brother who I taught to read when he was three, and maybe he had a point and I

11

should package my ideas as a management consultant would. I was tempted. But I argued that there were some 82,000 public schools, each serving a different population, and that I could only suggest ways to improve, not prescribe them.

To avoid the comparison, with horses and rabbits, I am offering seeds. Elizabeth T. Seabrook, who was enormously helpful reading and commenting as the book unfolded, supported the new title after she found this definition of seed in Webster's: "Teaching from which better conditions should develop."

Not only did Liz read the full manuscript and suggest clarifying editorial changes, but so did two master teachers, A. June Dickey and Jack Ragle.

From June: "Is it possible to implement the suggestions or are they air castles?" And from Jack: "What can you do so that your suggestions will be taken seriously?"

I am not building air castles. I do want to be taken seriously. And this book is chock full of seeds—of specific ways to improve teachers and principals and parents and school board members and teaching from which better conditions should develop. As June comments, answering her own question about air castles, "The road looks long, long. Cooperation seems to be the key with a strong sense of dedication."

Children are very precious to me. So is democracy. Adéle, one of the four teachers to whom "Seeds" is dedicated, used to ask, "Do you want to have or do you want to be?" What a profound question! Democracy is not something we have; it is what we are. It is the way we help our neighbors; it's our pursuit of happiness; it is our willingness to treat all others as equals; it's what we give our children as free education.

Let me explain why so many of the suggestions for improvement are presented in piecemeal fashion. Those requiring a whole new way of structuring schools and schooling, of dealing with teachers, of changing the curriculum, of rearranging what will be housed in school buildings, are introduced first when the ethos or general environment of free public schooling is discussed. Then these ideas are reintroduced and explored in more depth as they impact on the different elements which govern our schools.

To highlight some of the key suggestions, I have provided checklists at the close of the first five chapters, and a checklist index covering the entire book after Chapter Seven. By no means do I think these are the only ways to improve our schools, but I do believe they are important enough to be considered by all those who teach in or govern our public schools.

I am thrilled with the introductions provided for some of the chapters by some of the most distinguished educators working in the United States today. I am enormously grateful to them for reading advanced proofs, for writing their introductions, and for being willing to be included in a book so full of sometimes radical suggestions for reform.

I know they don't all agree with all the ideas for change; nor will you. But every one of these seeds deserves your consideration. We must love our children deeply enough—and unselfishly enough—to improve our schools, continuously.

Introduction to Chapter One

Improving the Ethos

By Harold Howe II

Senior Lecturer, Harvard Graduate School of Education
Cambridge, Massachusetts

In her opening chapter Cynthia Parsons starts with the right subject, the "ethos" of the school, as she calls it. This short word describes the most important aspect of a school—its climate, its atmosphere, its capacity to promote association among children and adults in ways to bring out the best in both and to make the school a place where respect, integrity, and affection set the tone for human relationship.

The "ethos" is more important than the school's curriculum or its organization, for it defines the main purpose of the school—providing a place where children can experience the meaning of democracy. All this sounds rather theoretical, and it even seems to go against standards of behavior and learning in the traditional sense. But when one reads the practical suggestions Cynthia Parsons makes for constructive ways of producing a positive school climate, those worries disappear. Here are day-to-day practices that can make a school vastly more effective, practices for teachers, parents, principals, janitors, and school officials. She doesn't tell all these people what to do. Instead, she provides them with an agenda for discussion in order to help them decide.

She provides them also with some challenging longer term thinking about how the school might become a vastly more effective institution in moving young people to maturity and into the workplace. Not all will embrace her concept of national service supervised by local high schools, but few will disagree with the objective she wants to reach, an improved sense of citizenship.

At the time I received the proof copy of Cynthia's book, her home State of Vermont was considering regulations to require schools to improve their "climate." Vermont might do better to send all its educators, parents, and school board members a complimentary copy of the first chapter of this book.

14

Chapter One

Improving the Ethos

It's a remarkable thing we do in the United States: We give every single child in our nation a minimum of ten years of free schooling.

We didn't always provide an education for every child. Some 100 years after the Declaration of Independence was signed, more than 80 percent of the children in the country weren't going to school. Instead, they were part of the labor force—generally doing those menial tasks adults didn't want to do. The 20 percent who were going to school had to pay for the privilege.

But by the time the United States observed its Bicentennial, every child in the nation had a free place in a public school. And a large percentage stayed in school after the age of 16 in order to earn a high school diploma.

All for free. All paid for by the public, and incredibly, mostly from self-imposed taxation. Today, the United States has more than 80,000 free public schools staffed by some 2.7 million educators, and attended by nearly 40 million pupils. Further, half the high school graduates go on to a college or university.

Yet, enormous criticism engulfs our schools. We're not satisfied; perhaps we never have been. There are those who so distrust the public schools that they promote schemes to channel public monies into private and independent schools so that our children won't have to attend our public schools.

But most Americans see our free public schools as a basic, fundamental, and inalienable provision for our children—to teach each one how to be a good citizen in a

15

strong democracy. And it's these concerned adults who want to strengthen and improve all U.S. public schools.

The parent asks: "How can I make school better for my child and for my neighbors' children?" The taxpayer questions spending priorities. The school board member asks where to turn to get expert and locally applicable advice.

And for every voice that argues that the public schools are "doomed" and not worth saving, ten voices are raised in protest and reform suggestions patter down on the schools like summer rain.

Where to begin? How to get some improvements started? Who should do what, when, and how often? Perhaps the logical place to start improving our schools is with their ethos, their character or fundamental spirit; that is, with the environment of each.

It's tempting to start off with a list of improvements concerned with size and organization, but I'll resist— saving those for later in this chapter—and wrestle, first, with the more intangible and subtle attitudes which separate good schools from bad schools; separate loving and productive atmospheres from prison-like encampments or holding areas.

Several recent education studies in England and the United States have focused in on ethos and environment—noting how changing the feeling and direction of a school can turn it from failing its pupils to providing them with the impetus to take the next step—be that more direct schooling or entry into the job market.

Schools do have feelings and attitudes; not only the sensitive visitor can feel the ethos, but so can all involved in creating that ethos. We can argue, and this book does, that principals have a lot to do with setting the tone of a school building. But so do teachers and janitors and students and uptown or downtown administrators, taxpayers, parents, school board members, city officials, legislators, and the state department of education.

To oversimplify one key environmental choice: Either public schools can be used by adults to separate children (a type of sorting mechanism), providing good instruction for the academically or technically inclined, and watered-down general studies for the "others;" or the public schools can be used to unify our children into that cadre prepared to carry on our great experiment in democracy—in which each man and woman is equal. At the very least our schools can provide each child with an equal opportunity during those compulsory (now ages 6–16) school years.

To oversimplify another key choice: Either our public schools can be used by adults to prepare children in lock-step annual moves for each next academic step, or they can be ends in themselves—providing youngsters with learning experiences associated with joy and fulfillment, self-esteem and self-expression.

And yet another choice: Adults can use schools as socio-economic selectors, based on socially contrived real estate patterns; or schools can be placed where every possible social level meets to learn how to be part of a greater whole—where ethnic, economic, religious, and cultural differences are admired and sustained, not neutralized.

Certainly, adults make the decision whether they consider all children basically evil and unruly, and see ten years of compulsory schooling as a time to impose arbitrary standards while expunging evil inclinations. There is more than a little evidence (the Gallup Poll is one source) that many adults want schools to be places where discipline is swift and punitive; where standards often not imposed in the home are to be enforced at school.

There are, of course, those adults who see all children as basically innocent; not evil. Who see them as eager to do and be right; as those who want love and respond to the same. Children who crave direction, welcome rules and regulations, understand fairness, but who despise the threatening rod, a police atmosphere, and discipline selectively administered.

It is the adults in a given community, and only slightly the children, who establish the ethos of a school. Adults decide what they want a school to be, what they want it to do, and how much of their resources they are willing to commit to it.

A substitute teacher spent a week in an inner-city middle school with a poor reputation. I asked him how the week went and what he thought of the school. "It's a prison run by the students."

No, he said, he would not go back; not for $100/day, much less the $35/day that city paid.

It would have taken something of a miracle to have made that school anything but a prison. It had been caught in the cross-fire of desegregation; was under court order, and not only had a hostile set of parents no other choice but to send their children to that school, but hostile teachers were assigned there against their wishes, the principal was on a one-year assignment, and police men and women regularly patrolled the halls.

No workshops were held to help the teachers understand how to deal with a different population from which they had ever been associated. Most of the teachers in the building had deliberately moved to a district outside the requirement of desegregation or sent their own children to a nonpublic school in order to avoid having their children be in a racially mixed environment.

There was no change in the curriculum to deal with the different social mix. No change in the lockstep approach to competitive academic classes. No change in the methods for teaching a wider range of entry abilities. No mechanisms were put in place to smooth out ethnic, racial, cultural, social, and economic differences. And those areas where differences could disappear—such as chorus, drama, folk dancing, museum field trips, etc.—were no part of this school's program.

But the miracle of change can happen. And has happened.

An elementary school principal in a Southern port city told me how she wept when she got her building assignment one spring and found she would be overseeing a 300–400-pupil, all-black elementary school "in one of the worst areas in town."

Further, since the school had had an all-black teaching staff, the "downtown" administrators had, without her consultation, removed half the black teachers and assigned white teachers (those with the least seniority) to fill their places.

There seemed little rhyme or reason to the choice of teachers moved in or out, until this experienced principal looked at their records and discovered that the "best trained" of the black teachers had been assigned out to formerly all-white schools and that she had not only inexperienced white teachers in half the classrooms, but apparently inferior black teachers in the other half.

She admitted that she had done little the first year except try to get herself reassigned to a school in one of the more affluent, all-white neighborhoods. And that she had encouraged the white teachers to form one social group and the black teachers another.

She explained that she didn't need to have two teachers' rooms, that she could so arrange free time that "it just fell out that way." Then came the testing program in the spring and her school's average scores in the 3 Rs were at the bottom within the school district.

She spent the next summer trying to get reassigned, to no avail. She started the second year's pre-school teachers' meeting by asking what they could do to raise the average to get off the bottom of the school-system list. A good many teachers, she explained, thought there wasn't anything they could do.

"Dumb kids = poor scores."

But then one teacher spoke up, admitting that these kids "are no dumber" than any others she'd taught.

"We still don't socialize outside school hours," the principal admitted, "but now we really get it together when we're in school."

And then she told me what she thought had changed the whole atmosphere. Many of the children in the neighborhood either were from single parent families or had both parents working. They were put out of their houses early; sometimes as much as an hour before school started. And when they got to school they were dirty, and their clothes were often wet.

The principal called on her own church group for secondhand pants and shirts; then when the children arrived with dirty, wet clothes, she got them to take a shower, put on clothes chosen from the box, put their own clothes in the washer/dryers she'd gotten a local laundry to donate, and come back at the end of the day to pick them up.

As she explained it, that broke the ice for the parents. They could come by school now and talk about how grateful they were for this service, and principal and parents had common ground for discussion—how in the world to keep an active 8-year-old clean and dry living on a dirt road next to a bayou.

And the teachers admitted that a cleaned-up pupil looked readier to learn the mysteries of long division than one squirming and smelling of swamp dirt.

A breakfast program was not long in coming to that school, courtesy of a lot of form filling-out by the now interested principal. Next was a way to accommodate parents who worked nights—they could have conferences during the day. And for those who worked days, they could come in the late evenings.

An active sports program was next, which required more group participation; lots of relay races and team activities. A buddy system by ability, and an attitude of the stronger helping the weaker took over.

From the principal: "If you had told me six years ago that I would fill out papers to keep me here; if you had tried to tell me six years ago that I wouldn't care about the color of the children, just whether they do what they're told or not; if you had told me six years ago that I'd break the school into learning groups instead of into grade levels . . . why I would have called you crazy."

She went on to say she had twice refused to be transferred. I asked how many of the inept teachers who were put in place that first year she'd been able to get rid of.

You all know how a stern principal looks when you've said something decidedly incorrect—well, that's the look she gave me for what seemed like eternity, and I suppose lasted three seconds. "They are all still here. Not a one of us wants out. They are the best teachers in this district."

She acknowledged that the two junior high schools to which her children went were not yet as "open" and "friendly" as her school, and that the children came back to complain. But she also agreed that it would be only a matter of time before the majority of the children in those junior highs would have come from her school, and that they would help "change that feeling from hurting to helping."

Hurting to helping—that's probably the difference between a learning and a non-learning environment.

Doing Chores

There are some marvelous feelings that can ooze from a school where every single pupil has a daily chore to do— something which helps to keep the environment clean and attractive.

In primary and elementary schools, these chores must of necessity be menial, but they are nonetheless important. The picking up of trash, the taking of waste baskets to a central location. The washing of windows, floors, walls, desks, tables, chairs. The running of errands, making of copies, helping younger children clean up after finger painting.

Playground maintenance, storeroom organizing, distribution of messages, cleaning of chalkboards. And on and on. The clever teacher—in conjunction with the principal and the custodial staff—can think of at least as many chores as pupils. Can organize older children, as their chore, to supervise younger children.

And the doing of such chores, particularly for junior and senior high youngsters can pull a whole school together into a working team, can cut down on vandalism, can promote discipline and orderliness.

Most of the public schools I have ever visited have chore lists, but for only a handful of students, and generally these duties are reserved for the "better" kids. Most of the nonpublic schools I have ever visited have chore lists, and often these include every single pupil. The name may be different: work activities, job time, activity period, and the like. But the idea is for much of the work around the school to be done by the pupils, not just for cutting down expenses, but also to teach lessons in thrift, orderliness, leadership, service, and to create that all-important ethos—happiness through togetherness.

Some wonderful feelings come from everyone having a chore—from doing that chore; being praised for doing it well; even learning from the letdown when the chore has been neglected. Curious that so many public schools, knowing how badly urban and suburban children need this kind of daily work experience, so often neglect to include chores in the curriculum.

If doing a chore regularly and well can teach self-reliance and promote responsible citizenship, why on earth would a school—whose very purpose is to develop good citizens—deliberately organize school days and weeks without the doing of menial jobs by the students?

Why, if we know it's true that teenagers will respect property they have helped to maintain, do we spend millions to repair vandalism and next to nothing for providing daily chores for all secondary school students?

And chores are a perfect area for dividing up youngsters differently from academic levels. The very boy or girl who finds reading a chore will be able to oil and repair audio-visual equipment with ease. While the "all thumbs" academician will have to sweep the gym floor, since he or she can't handle a more technical assignment.

And chores are a good way to divide the school into ageless teams. Let the older and wiser supervise the younger.

And further, chores done should be reported. Here, again, is an opportunity for a school to run on its own efficiency, for pride in accomplishment to be a daily recognition, and hence for the ethos of that institution to sparkle with a cooperative camaraderie, not crackle with tension built on competition and a type of survival of the fittest.

Keeping in Touch

There are very few professionals in white-collar jobs throughout our whole industrial/technological economy who are without access to a telephone. Certainly those professional workers whose jobs require them to keep in touch with at least 25 contacts on a regular basis would have phones in their offices.

And certainly there are few professional jobs where telephone access to supervisory personnel or for consultation to experts is so difficult to come by as in our public schools.

Our school teachers need office space, or in the modern jargon, work stations. The space may be nothing more than a partitioned corner of a classroom, but there each teacher should have a telephone. And they should be expected to use this link with all parents and guardians, and also with those other professionals who can provide help as needed.

As school buildings get emptier, partitions can create work stations for all professional staff in the building, and phone links are essential.

Do you know a large school building whose custodian has not framed for himself an office complete with telephone? It is one of the many ironies of many visits to hundreds of secondary schools—big important plants full of highly degreed professionals, almost none of whom has access to a private desk area. Go tour the basement, and there's usually a complete office set-up. Yes, the custodian needs a phone, but so do the teachers.

Upstairs in the same school, there may be a teacher who has a pupil quarantined at home and missing algebra. The teacher has no access to that pupil, but both clearly would welcome keeping in touch. How convenient for the algebra teacher to do this while the class was in session.

And while we're on the subject of phones, let's not overlook the need for junior and senior high schools to have banks of pay phones for use by students. Working parents and school-going teenagers need to keep in touch; need to work out complicated family schedules. And the 1,000-pupil school with two pay phones located in the rain and sleet sends a shiver down the "ethos" back of sensitivity.

We love our children; we love their need of privacy; and we want to encourage their sense of responsibility. We must provide them with the tools to be responsible and responsive. Hence, for every 25 students in a secondary school, at least one telephone.

And in the elementary, primary, and middle schools,

why not have a community volunteer oversee a phone for every 50 children. These pupils, too, need to be in touch with home parents as well as with working parents. And they may need to talk over what they want to call about with a helpful adult so that the message sent is clear and accurate.

Small Size Makes a Big Difference

I asked the head of psychological services for a 20,000-pupil school district how big a school building should be, and he didn't hesitate with his answer: "five hundred for junior and senior highs, and 300 for elementary schools."

We're talking about just 10–12 years of a person's life; but in many ways among the most important years of a lifetime. Here in these school years, basic lessons in how to learn are established. Somehow the "feeling" of the school must promote learning how to learn. Somehow the atmosphere of the school must set the tone for 60 or 70 more years of learning and knowing how to use what one has learned.

There is hardly an educator to be found who would argue that a secondary school should be larger than 1,000 pupils; and no scholar who thinks 300 pupils in the lower grades is too few.

Yet, right across the United States we built too big. And while we may have tried to save money doing so, we really didn't—particularly when we ignored the cost for heating, lighting, and air conditioning large-scale school buildings.

But one marvelous way to improve our schools is to use those big buildings in exciting and imaginative ways. Scale down to 500 or 300 pupils. Then:

Put a preschool (or daycare center) in every building.

Put a branch of the local public library in every building.

Put neighborhood and town social agencies in every building.

Put a substation of the state or local police in every building.

Put a health clinic in every building.

Put a senior center in every building; use the school cafeteria for whatever free or subsidized meals are served in town.

Turn many of the smaller classrooms or divide larger ones into music practice rooms and rent to all interested musicians in town; add a kiln or two near the art rooms and permit a local potter to rent space.

Ask the local museum to reserve a hallway for display space in special cabinets.

House the town recreation committee; house social clubs; house such public groups as Boy and Girl Scouts; place a branch of the YM or YWCA in an area of the school.

Allow private, non-profit dance, drama, literary, and athletic clubs to rent appropriate space.

What a wonderful school that would be which housed so many different activities; which had so many caring and thoughtful adults going in and out each day, which could offer pupils mentors, counselors, and examples from within the building!

And think what it would mean if the menial chores for all these groups were done by the pupils in the building under supervision first of pupils and ultimately of the concerned adults! That would make chore-doing worthwhile. It would make chore-doing seem like the activity it should be—part of the daily round of joy for each worker in our society.

Margaret Mead, addressing the National Association of Independent Schools, berated them for limiting their campuses to such a narrow age band instead of including a fuller spectrum. She argued that some way should be found, particularly in day schools, to have grandparents as well as infants not only seen but heard.

For every public school to house an active preschool, and to offer activities for senior citizens, is to make our schools more life-like, and hence improve the impact they have on our lives.

For these improvements to take place, parents and citizens must become more involved in decision-making at the local school level. The public schools are our schools.

It's our provision for our children—our provision to help them develop into productive adults with enough academic and skill background to be able to choose a healthy way of life.

Of course, those directly involved with running schools, have an enormous amount to do with the ethos of each school, but so do the rest of us. It's noted that more than 75 percent of all taxpayers do not have children in school; some would suggest this is one reason school budgets fail to pass in local elections.

But talks with older citizens reveal not so much an unwillingness to help pay for schooling for the community's children as it is a concern in two important directions: (1) that those running the schools are not being fiscally prudent and economizing at every turn; and (2) that the school is not demanding enough of the pupils either in their behavior patterns or in their academic courses.

Letting the Community Help

Certainly the senior citizens who regularly used school facilities for activities, and who had their housekeeping chores done by the children, and who could participate in watching little plays and skits, listening to singing, hearing children read, watching scientific experiments develop, would be eager to see that the school was well financed and equipped.

Those artists in town who had an opportunity to work with school youngsters, and to see how well they maintained their school and its artistic equipment, would be thrilled to support higher taxes knowing it would improve an already good institution.

Those working parents, with precious little time to make school visits, would respond warmly to hearing regularly by phone from each teacher; would be much more interested in working out ways for homework to be supervised if necessary, but certainly scheduled as needed, if they were in constant touch with a helpful teacher who not only knew their child well, but cared as they did about the development of that child as a learner.

Of course, parents can do much to improve the ethos of a school. One has only to see what a difference it makes to young athletes when the playing field is surrounded by appreciative adults; when the gym on a winter's evening has a strong cheering section; when the science fair has a steady throng of interested adults; when plays have an audience; and school musicians are invited to perform for community groups.

The artist who gives a painting to a school; the sculptor who donates a piece of work; the musician who offers to give a performance; the businessman who is willing to supervise a senior project; the store manager who is willing to hire and supervise those interested in a sales career; the author who is willing to talk with the group putting out this year's literary yearbook; the citizen who is willing to be a big brother or sister; the retired teacher who is willing to tutor—this list is endless. It fills out as a town fills out. It grows as the school environment welcomes and seeks such growth.

A good many schools have already found a way to tap community resources; with the help of concerned parents they make an inventory of what is available. And should a teacher, studying the mammals of South America, for example, want and need an expert in that field, the inventory gives all the necessary data to bring a photojournalist, or travelling mammalogist, or amateur natural scientist just back from a visit to Latin America to school for a talk or slide show or movie or . . .

There are more than 3,000 college and universities across the United States. It is not unreasonable to estimate that some 9,000 of the 82,000 public schools in the United States are located near an institution of higher learning. So?

For every pupil in those 9,000 schools who could use some tutoring in basic skills, there is an undergraduate more than willing to do the tutoring. For every pupil who has a special hobby or interest, there is an undergraduate with the same hobby or interest willing to spend special time as a mentor to a neophyte.

For the pupils in the other 73,000 schools, there are such

mentors in the community—just waiting to be asked to help out at the local school.

Is there a child with a handicap? Surely an adult who has long since learned to cope with such a handicap would be willing to be a mentor, a counselor, a sympathizer, a teacher.

It's often hard to tell, when able children work with their handicapped peers for some special event, who is more thrilled by the encounter. The able child often will remember the occasion for the rest of his life, feeling over and over again the thrill of being able to make such a big difference in the life of another.

Is there a child with a special talent? Certainly there is at least one person who understands that talent and can provide ways to nourish and strengthen it.

Is there a student who wants to learn an exotic language? Doesn't the community include at least one person skilled in that language? And couldn't the school arrange for lessons?

Working to make such marvelous encounters happen is the work of both citizens and educators. There are a great many adults whose working lives do not permit them to help children in school during school hours. But there are many who can. Perhaps it's initially up to the school to seek them out.

But experience shows that once the school reaches out, then parents and townspeople reach out as well. Let a school seem like a comfortable place for adults of all kinds to be, and the school will be rich and full. Let the school be stiff and unyielding, and it's hard to get anyone to come to even the parent-teacher organization meeting.

As many who have tried to work with school administrators well know, many a teacher and principal thinks parents should be seen and not heard. Where that is the modus operandi, generally the school is unfit for the children assigned to it. That's even more reason for citizens and parents to come to school in droves, to work for a more healthy, healing, and happy environment.

The saying goes that parents send the best children they

have to school; it follows that school districts staff the same schools with the best teachers they have.

But even the best can be made better, and it's the very ethos of desire to be better which is needed.

Starting School When Ready

We've been admitting little children into our schools in a very curious manner. No matter how ready a five- or six-year-old is, we only allow children to start grade one in late August or early September. This places with one teacher (the jargon is a self-contained classroom) some 25, 30, or even 35 pupils, all of whom are rank beginners. Because we've been doing things this way for so many years, college students intending to become teachers are trained in methods for dealing with a whole classroom full of beginners.

But a few schools have discovered that family groupings (children aged five, six, seven, and eight) work much better; also as soon as a little five-year-old exhibits the maturity and interest to spend a day in a school setting, they come along. It might be January 3 for a precocious five-year-old and May 17 for a quieter child.

And as the little ones fit into a school setting, they are placed in a classroom with a grouping of children each of whom is at a different stage of basic skill development. This gives each adult teacher a group of pupils to help out. And it means that a teacher probably doesn't have to deal with more than ten rank beginners at any one time.

What generally happens is that a child, soon after the fifth birthday, pays a visit to school and is "tested" for maturity. The tester—perhaps a special counselor, maybe one of the teachers, often the principal—decides which "family" this little one should join for a day or two. This testing of the school "waters" may be followed by once-a-week visits, and with many conferences between the teacher and the parents. Suggestions are made about how the home can help the maturing child; how to ready each child for a schoolroom experience.

Together home and school work out a schedule which aids everyone concerned. Then comes the day that it's all day for the pupil, then all week, and finally enrollment full time. By this time, both the teacher and the older pupils in the room are well acquainted with the newcomer; further, there is a group of older children ready and willing to help teach the beginner.

In some schools that use this type of grouping, children might remain with the same teacher for more than a year; in other schools, the pupils are grouped and regrouped frequently by ability and interest and in accordance with which teachers work best with which pupils.

Competition in such a setting is almost extinct. Instead, cooperation reigns. The teacher who can handle this 25–30-ring circus wouldn't be restricted to the self-contained classroom ever again; and the teacher used to handling a one-age, one-grade group may need at least a year under the tutelage of an expert before leaving the lockstep for the spontaneous.

Interestingly enough, more educators than parents seem willing to give this more hospitable school environment a try. And particularly to go down yet another year and offer schooling to four-year-olds. We have been so wedded to the lockstep approach, and so many of us have been through it with some success, that we're dumbfounded at the suggestion that children should ignore the calendar and instead go to school the week they are ready for school. Ready, that is, in the combined eyes of the parents, the child, and the school.

What schools might do is to turn several classrooms into family groups, and leave one set of classes in the old self-contained mode. Let parents sit in on both; let the children visit both. Then let parents and pupils choose which for a semester at a time.

A teacher I talked with in a "continuous progress" school, who had stuck with a fifth-grade class, said she had been given a sabbatical and, further, that she was going to spend it in her own school as a teacher's aide in a "family" room. What do you think will happen? I asked.

She smiled: "I know what will happen. I'll be hooked and never look back." I pressed for a why. She was quiet for a moment, and then admitted, "We always claim we're starting where the child is, and then start where the book does. If it's really continuous progress, then we really ought to start where the pupils are."

Dancing To Start the Day

Dance is a marvelous activity, particularly folk dancing. It's not only good exercise, but it's socializing as well. Further, it promotes good listening and develops physical coordination. Beauty, grace, and symmetry characterize dancers—all qualities which make for a gracious school.

What a wonderful way to start a school day! And why not let parents who have the time and inclination join in with beginning-of-the-school-day dancing? Many folk dances are best done by mixed ages and sizes, again giving a school an opportunity to break down those artificial age barriers.

A work day that starts with song and laughter, and stretches some muscles, lends itself later to seat work—reading, writing, and quantitative thinking.

A school that's filled with song and dance has got to be a happy one; the ethos has to be conducive to good feeling, to productivity, to a healthful joy.

A great many boys and girls, particularly during the early teens, would love to be able to dance instead of doing gymnastics or playing volleyball. Why not include dance as physical education? Why not let language classes teach foreign-language folk songs to other classes as part of their school assignment?

And why not let song be an active part of the school? What about having one class group serenade another? What about one class group writing one verse of a song and then challenging another class to do the second? What about adults in the community, free during school hours, joining in to swell a chorus and mix mature voices with the very young?

A school where dancing and singing figure prominently and spontaneously in each day's activities would not be one where a visitor would hear silence in the halls.

There are many ways to include more of the older members of the community in school activities. And by so doing, a balance and perspective contribute to a school's healthy learning environment. One way is to invite senior citizens with a skill to come and share with one or two pupils. Maybe it's nothing more than a love of putting together picture puzzles. Couldn't a room be cleared for this for a half hour each day and let little ones work with the elderly until all the pieces fit?

And what about all the senior knitters, crocheters, tatters, hand weavers, and stitchers? Wouldn't they love to come to school for a short time each day (or week) and work with interested boys and girls informally wherever they could find a nook?

There's something else the older folks can do; they can listen to beginning readers who want to read or to tell a story. No teacher has enough ears to listen to as many children as want and need to be heard. Why not enlist someone's grandparents to help do the listening?

Certainly the feeling of a school will change dramatically if older people are coming and going all day long, each one working with one or two interested children. And a little handicraft work, sandwiched between more cerebral activities, can only help make the environment happy and productive.

Our schools really can be full of joy; full of adventure; full of those who love being there and love sharing what they know.

It's curious, too, that so many of our schools run on such rigid rules that courtesy is not a regular and conscious way of life. Harsh bells ring regardless of where one is in a lesson; school-wide sound systems intrude when least expected (or wanted). In many city schools, guards patrol the halls and all classroom doors are shut and locked. Even the door to the outside is locked, and visitors must pass through guards and metal detectors to gain entrance.

Courtesy Is Essential

Oh, but a courteous school is a healthy school and a healthy school is a learning environment.

A math specialist—a college professor—began trying some math lessons in a particularly unruly junior high. He dropped a piece of chalk and a child sprang forward to pick it up. As he did so, this gentle man said "thank you." The boy gave him a startled look; and so the professor repeated his courtesy, adding "thank you for getting the piece of chalk."

The boy almost smirked as he explained: "I have to do it, the teacher told me to."

Sensing the undercurrent of hostility, the professor readdressed the boy: "Nevertheless, I am grateful to you, and once again want to thank you for picking up the chalk."

It was not long before the lad got a chance to return the courtesy. Behind him in the class was a gum-popping girl who was chatting with a neighbor. The chalk boy turned around and asked them to be quiet. "Teacher's pet" was the rejoinder.

The math teacher intervened: "You girls may talk if you wish; I'm just sorry this lesson does not interest you. It's obviously my fault." He wasn't grinning, nor did the girls feel any cynicism. What they heard was genuine . . . the good Ph.D. was sorry he couldn't interest them in what consumed most of his waking hours.

The lad could bear it no longer. "Excuse me, sir, the problem is you went too fast over that last point and they got lost. May I fill them in?"

Now it was time for the regular classroom teacher to nearly faint dead away. This was the class bully; this was the chronic troublemaker. And courtesy had managed more than scores of trips to the principal's office.

In a one-room schoolhouse, even though the teacher has been in close proximity all day with fewer than 20 pupils, nevertheless the teacher, at the close of each school day, shakes hands with each one as they leave. A special word is exchanged, and often this teacher thinks of something that has happened during the day for which she can be sincerely grateful.

A math teacher arranged his classes in rows (he had no choice as the desks were nailed to the floor) with a leader at the front of each. It was the leader's job to move quietly up and down the row making sure that every pupil understood the directions. Politeness and courtesy were the order of the day. It came directly from the teacher. He treated a failure as a delightful opportunity for him to think of yet another way to get a math concept across to eager students.

In a large secondary school, where about 20 percent of the students were physically handicapped, the teachers and administrators led the way, allowing each pupil to make his way through the school and the school day at his own pace. Pupils who were in wheelchairs were not to be pushed; blind children were not to be guided; deaf children were not to be ignored. Instead, teachers and student leaders thought of ways to help the handicapped be independent; and those with the special needs thought of ways they could say thank you.

Perhaps one of the most difficult places within the school environment to bring a feeling of grace and instill natural courtesy is the cafeteria during the noon-hour rush! This seems particularly true in elementary schools. And even more true in cafeterias policed by "lunch ladies" who often terrorize the children into a semblance of silence.

School lunchrooms don't have to have this chaotic feeling. One solution, of course, is to include parents and older citizens in the lunch program. Another is to relax rules about sharing among children. Another is to ask the pupils to be menu designers; to include them in choosing meals to be served. Another is to have every pupil, on a rotating basis, handle some of the lunchroom chores, including some of the serving activities.

I have visited several schools where a section of the auditorium is roped off at noon for those with bag lunches, and while in there, the students listen to classical music. In other schools, a group of ladies arrive at noon with a hot meal, put table cloths down, and serve the children in one room and school staff in another. At a few schools, teachers sit at the head and foot of lunch tables, serve plates with heaping as well as "no-thank-you" helpings, and generally maintain an air of civility and courtesy throughout the meal.

Of course, courtesy must start with the adults in the school; this means that children have to be treated civilly, and that cynicism must not be allowed to govern teacher-pupil relationships.

School restrooms are another place where the ethos needs improving. Again, permitting students, on a rotating basis, to be the ones to clean the bathrooms will do much for their cleanliness and for keeping them free of smokers, dopers, and deviants. A bathroom which is checked at least once an hour and at random times, and where the checker is also the cleaner, is definitely going to be cleaner and freer of "funny business" than one which is inhabited all day by students and only after school hours by custodial staff.

It may be necessary in some schools for all the adults in the building to use the student bathrooms. In this way, adult checks provide a balance for student checks, and, again, proper use of such a facility is enhanced. Today, in most schools, student bathrooms are not supervised, not used by the adults in the building, are not cleaned regularly by students, and hence become "secret" meeting places for those intent on doing mischief.

Finding Reasons for Praise

Perhaps this is a good place to discuss the giving of awards. It's curious that more schools don't recognize how very much an award means to a child, and how much pleasure an award can give a struggling child. For a few children, school activities come naturally. But for most children, the majority of what's required to succeed in school is somewhat alien, and enormous energy and devotion to task is required. Awards for efforts expended as well as for achievements earned might provide some children with a much-needed impetus.

In one school, the principal roved the halls looking for a pupil who was spontaneously doing something positive. Up came the camera, and an instant picture was taken. Identification of the subject was next, and then all was posted in the main hall for everyone to see and admire.

A teacher in the elementary grades strung string across the room just above the head height of the children. Construction paper was stapled together and hung from the lines. Every single time a pupil did something "special" or particularly worthwhile, down came a strip of construction paper, on went the name of the pupil in big block letters, and up it went again for all the world to see. Pupils could nominate each other for these awards, and as the school year progressed if one or more children didn't get their names hung up, the whole class worked with them to help them do something especially worthy.

Because schooling is compulsory, and because we've used schools as sorting devices—unfortunately, as much for social as academic reasons—we've caused a significant proportion of the population to hate schools, school buildings, teachers, and administrators. We tend to want to argue that the problem is with the haters, and not ever so directly connected to the ethos or feeling we school people have deliberately created.

But, we're really to blame when 20 boys and girls throw 100 rocks through 40 school windows; when rampaging students break open the fire-hose cabinets and turn on the water at midnight; when broken glass is scattered all over the locker room floor; when butter pats are splattered on the cafeteria ceiling; when the seat cushions in the auditorium are gouged out; when a crayon is stuffed in a pencil sharpener; when gangs form and fight in halls and on the playground.

Why are we to blame for the discourteous and unruly behavior of a few students? Why are we to blame for the rude actions and near criminal behavior of non-students?

Because we adults—particularly those of us trusted with running our schools—set the tone for how every child and young adult in town is treated. We set the tone for how each youngster is to be trained, schooled, and educated. And those who are in school, as well as those who have dropped or been pushed out, are extremely sensitive to that tone. What ethos is projected has a lot to do with how every child in town thinks about himself/herself. The school's mental environment either supports or ridicules those who are its users.

Much is made of the fact that nonpublic schools can put out of their community whichever pupils they don't want there; also they can select only those whom they want. And since the school has the choice, it can control—better than any free public school—the environment. Heads of private schools who have come from the public sector often will speak of this controlling difference and make the point that being able to be selective "makes this job easier."

Yet the more sensitive school administrator will admit that the problem is usually with the school; it has in its own way failed to meet the needs of the pupil it must expel. There are very rare instances when the child's problem is really insurmountable, and when the school's resources are inadequate to deal with the peculiar circumstances.

But the nonpublic schools are onto something very important with their reasoning: They are admitting that their mental atmosphere comes from their own collective thinking, and, further, that often that atmosphere is very limited. That they are so inflexible that the pupil must be the one to fit in or they will put the pupil out.

This is not what democracy is all about. This is not what's meant by giving every one of us an equal opportunity at the starting gate of adulthood.

And the public schools of the United States must create a quite different environment: a helping, healing, successful one. Not forever, just for 10 years on a compulsory basis and as many as 12 or 13 on a voluntary basis.

Co-op Instead of Voc Ed

It's true, we should probably start formal schooling at age 4, and we also should expect children to complete "basic training" (I couldn't resist the phrase, sorry) by the age of 14. For a few youngsters, what would come next would be more schooling. For some, straight academics with an eye eventually to a profession—doctor, lawyer, merchant, chief.

For some, schooling in a vocation or industry. And at this point, all such training would be what is called "cooperative education." In co-op ed, students alternate periods of study with periods of work in a related job. Both the job supervisor and the school trainer share responsibility for guiding and grading the student.

In this way, we can imagine Jack and Jill graduating from high school at age 14, after spending ten straight years in the classroom. Then Jack and Jill would return to the local high school and work out with the school authorities what job-related schooling they would take in conjunction with a part-time job. The program can vary with the needs of the employer: Students might spend half a day in school and half on the job; a week in school and a week on the job; a term in school and a term on the job.

One of the simpler ways schools have worked this out is to place two students from the same school in one job slot, and while one is at school the other is holding down the job. This covers that job slot for the employer and permits the school to have double the enrollment using half the space, while providing instructors with smaller classes.

We now have a picture of a school system which is deliberately preparing its pupils for one of two possibilities after the ten compulsory basic years. One, the pupil graduates and goes into a post-secondary school—college, university, institute, or what have you. Two, the pupil returns to the school for two years of cooperative education training for a specific skill (and simultaneous practice of that skill) for the next two years.

Now, this means that each high school is responsible for

each graduate. There is no room in this suggested improvement for the school to graduate, expel, or watch leave all of its students—regardless of the level of their school success—claiming that they have no further responsibility for them. Instead, each youngster would either be succeeding in the post-secondary school of his/her choice, or would be involved in a cooperative education program under the high school's guidance.

It is not hard to imagine what an impetus this cadre of students (alternating school with a paying job) would be to those younger children coming up through the basic academics. They would be housed in the same building, guided by the same administrators, taught by many of the same teachers, and share the same atmosphere of success.

The reader of this volume might well wonder what schools are now doing—if they are not already too well aware—for those who leave at 16 or graduate. A few do take co-op ed or some type of vocational training. Another few prepare rigorously for post-secondary schooling, some of whom are admitted to the college of their choice. But an enormous number of students leave their compulsory years of schooling with neither the required college-preparatory training nor with proven job-skill training.

There aren't many of these students leaving Scarsdale High, or Palo Alto, or Boston Latin, but hundreds of thousands leave rural, inner-city, and even many suburban high schools without sufficient schooling and with no ties to the school which was supposed to prepare them for adult democracy.

By each community's saying to its children that they will either be fitted to go immediately on to college or be given two years of job training, the adults in town say, effectively, we love you and we want you to join us in growing and producing and succeeding.

Giving Two Years of National Service

But our schools should do more than just get children ready for jobs and college—we need to get them ready to be an active part of our democracy. Every young person in our nation should give two years of service to the country.

Two years sometime between the ages of 16 and 26. And the young people should have their choice, not only of which two years to give to national service, but the type of service as well. For a great many, the choice will be service with the armed forces. Another large portion will undoubtedly choose to serve locally in the social service sector or in civil government.

And a minority will want to serve overseas in diplomatic and peace corps-type activities.

For a good many young people, the school system will be an obvious place to give two years of service, providing each school in the United States with interested aides, with teachers' helpers, with coaches for both academics and athletics, with mentors, counselors, role models.

The young man or woman who has gone from high school direct to college and then to law school might save his/her national service until the close of law school, and then spend the two years in a public defender's office. Or, after making the decision to go on to law school after completing undergraduate work, the young adult might choose to do two years of national service in a justice department, in an effort to discover just what area of the law he or she wants most to specialize in.

For the pre-med student, two years of national service in a local health and welfare program might signal the area of medicine most desired by this particular student; or the two years of national service might come at the close of training in medicine and be considered part of the internship in cases where the work is in the public and not the private sector.

But even more important than the concept of two years of public service for every young adult is the renewed purpose this gives our public schools. It is they who should be the guardians and trackers of this service. It is our public schools which should have as one of their major purposes the preparing of young people for this service time.

We've treated our children quite shamefully for almost four generations—giving them schooling not directly connected to the purpose of that schooling. This explains why recent study after study records so much mediocrity and why so many drop out before completing high school. In order for the ethos of the school to support those within the school, each would have to know the purpose of the school.

And those who would argue that nonpublic schools somehow "do a better job" have their finger on an important pulse. Yes, most private schools have a clear and single purpose; certainly those which are college preparatory select only those who they think will get to college, drop along the way those who might not make the goal, and hence, if the success count is based on what percent of the graduates go on to further education, a prep school can beat a general purpose public school every time.

Preparing for Democracy

But our public schools have a broader trust, a more important purpose, a more precious constituency, a more difficult task. Yes, they have got to prepare some students for college and some for jobs, but further they must prepare us all for democracy. Must prepare us for a world of service, of caring, and of healing. We're the leaders of the free world. Not a selection of us, but all of us together.

Our schools provide the start for that leadership, and preparing us all for two years of service is the most natural activity in the world. It's also self-fulfilling, since much of the service will be done right in the school settings and in local parks and playgrounds.

Picture, if you will, a city or town where everyone between the ages of 4 and 14 is in school daily; then where about half those between the ages of 14 and 16 are spending part of their time in school and part in a job, while they live at home. Further, about a fourth of the youngsters between the ages of 14 and 18 would be in college, some locally and others off in another community.

Then, too, there would be youngsters anywhere between the ages of 16 and 26 around the area providing services to the community—services which all those up to the age of 16 understand they will one day be "privileged" to perform. And whether national service is a privilege or a "pain" will devolve heavily on those who run our public schools.

But, of course, they, too, would have come along the same route (it will take a generation for this to take place) and probably would have followed a path like one of these:

Ages 4–14	—	In school
Ages 14–16	—	In cooperative education
Ages 16–18	—	In national service
	or	
Ages 4–14	—	In school
Ages 14–18	—	In college/university
Ages 18–20	—	In national service
	or	
Ages 4–14	—	In school
Ages 14–18	—	In college/university
Ages 18–21	—	In graduate school
Ages 21–24	—	In a job
Ages 24–26	—	In national service

Think of the wonderful improvements in our schools as we all agreed on a central purpose for them; as we all worked together to create both a beautiful and workable physical plant, but even more importantly a magnificent mental atmosphere where every child really did get the guidance and training particularly suited to his needs. As we, at the same time, kept in place our nation's unique offering of higher education to every single person who wants it regardless of background. From early admissions for those with exceptional academic talent to the senior citizens in the Elder Hostel program, learning and degree-earning are not limited to a select few of our population. They are free to whomever.

Certainly this generous provision for higher education signals to elementary and secondary schools what their special purpose is, and the improvements suggested throughout the following chapters—some costly and others modest in the extreme—are designed to help us move toward schools which teach. Toward good schools. Toward purposeful schools.

Checklist

1. *Chores:* A daily chore for every pupil supervised by older students complete with daily written reports.

2. *Phones:* A phone and office space for every teacher to be used to keep in constant contact with out-of-school pupils and with parents. A generous number of pay phones for the use of pupils.

3. *Size:* No more than 500 pupils enrolled in a junior or senior high; no more than 300 in an elementary school. Fill additional space with daycare programs as well as compatible non-profit agencies and institutions.

4. *Volunteers:* Let community volunteers help with reading, listening, singing, dancing, teaching, showing, encouraging. . . .

5. *September:* Don't have first graders start school only in September, but any time during the school year so that teachers will get them when they are ready, and only have a handful of rank beginners at any one time.

6. *Dancing:* Start the school day with folk dancing and singing; let parents and other community members join in; let dancing be part of physical education.

7. *Courtesy:* A polite and gracious principal leading polite and gracious staff and teachers encouraging pupils to be polite and gracious.

8. *Praise:* Find reasons to give awards to each and every pupil.

9. *Age 4:* That's the year to start school—sometime between a child's fourth and fifth birthdays when the three parties agree—the school, the parents, and the child.

10. *National Service:* Let every young adult sometime between the ages of 16 and 26 give two years of service to our nation supervised by local public high schools.

11. *Democracy:* Determine that the purpose of our

schools is to prepare youngsters not necessarily for a job or college, but for active participation in our democracy.

School superintendents: You're going to have to lead the way on this business of improving the feeling and environment of a school. After all, you are responsible for placing principals and hiring faculty and staff. And for every improvement which is tried, there are parent and citizen groups who will demand an explanation from you. You, for example, cannot believe that children are basically evil, and at the same time put the children first when developing a curriculum. Nor can you be a racist, and at the same time help the schools adjust to both an integrated student body and a racially mixed faculty.

School board members and trustees: A good many of these improvements require your leadership. If we're going to stop using schools as dividers and sorters, if we're going to accept children as innocent and responsive and treat them accordingly, if we're going to adjust the curriculum to fit the needs of the students and not the other way around, if teachers are to have phones and offices, if school building space is to be rented out to daycare and other compatible agencies, and so forth, you will have to direct the superintendent, the principals, and the teachers to carry out these changes.

Principals, teachers, aides, secretaries, coaches, janitors, teacher interns: Perhaps you think you already look for ways to help and not hurt each other and the pupils. But maybe the hurts are there and you just haven't noticed them; maybe the helps don't begin to cancel out the pain. You're the ones to know; the ones to know how much it would mean to children to put on fresh clothes, to have full tummies, to be able to do a chore and win an award for so doing. And you're certainly going to have to lead the way to keep enrollment per building below 500 pupils, and to fill school buildings with all types of social and civic agencies.

Parents: Do you know that you're often seen as the No. 1 obstruction to progress, particularly in our U.S. public schools? No way should you stand in the way of improvements; you have the most to gain from the highest quality schools. You have very little to gain from trying to arrange good schooling for your children and inferior schooling for everyone else's children. What's best for your children is best for all. The above checklist is a good one to use when deciding which school is best for your children; also good to use after you've chosen and become intimately interested in improvements.

Improving Teachers

by Mary Hatwood Futrell
President, National Education Association
Washington, D.C.

I have taught in the public schools of Virginia for 20 years. As president of the National Education Association, I've criss-crossed our great country and visited classrooms in nearly every state. I've spoken with teachers at every level of our schools, in every discipline.

The typical American teacher? I'm convinced that there isn't one. But I do believe that the overwhelming majority of my colleagues share a common commitment to doing their best.

Why then, I'm often asked, aren't there more "quality" teachers? Why aren't teachers "better"? Good questions. But these questions can't be answered without understanding what our educational system does to teachers.

Today's educational system actually discourages teachers from pursuing quality. It's a system that prepares prospective teachers for the classroom by force-feeding them teacher educa-tion courses that divorce teaching theory from teaching practice. It's a system that drops young teachers into overcrowded class-rooms with outdated textbooks—and fills teachers' days with bus duty, attendance-taking, and a million other time-wasting tasks that have nothing to do with teaching.

And when teachers' performance comes up short, our na-tional leaders ignore these obstacles—*and* teachers' opinions—and instead propose politically popular and educationally inane panaceas like merit pay and prayer in the schools. Meanwhile, at the same time, school officials refuse to fund and administer the rigorous evaluation systems that would truly help teachers become better teachers.

Why do teachers accept these obstacles? They don't. In every school district I've ever visited, teachers are rejecting the conditions that discourage quality teaching. They're struggling for time to teach and plan, for adequate class sizes, for up-to-date textbooks and well-equipped laboratories, for meaningful teacher education and in-service programs, for a say in the decisions that shape our schools.

As a teacher, I welcome ideas to improve my profession. But I have little patience for gameplans to improve teaching that ignore basic questions of educational finance. Teachers need more than laundry lists of "bright ideas." We need concrete budget resources for equipment, for textbooks, for classroom aides, for remedial and enrichment programs, for salaries that don't insult teachers with every paycheck.

With this support, my colleagues and I can work learning miracles. Without it, the daily frustrations of contemporary classroom life will continue to grind away the love of learning that attracts young men and women into teaching.

Chapter Two
Improving Teachers

What one factor—above all others—is the key to a good school?

Teachers and teaching.

Prevailing wisdom says you can have a crumbling building, a corrupt school board, an apathetic or cost-cutting community and still produce educated pupils if (granted it's a huge if) you have superb teachers.

Conversely, your building may be elegant and have well-equipped labs and Olympic-size swimming pools, the principal may be known throughout the state for his innovative ideas, the school board may be conscientious about holding meetings, and the community willing to tax itself "to the limit," but if several of the teachers are mean, intellectually dishonest, or ill-prepared, then good schooling doesn't exist there for scores of students.

Heads of selective private schools know this about their teaching staffs; the better ones go to considerable lengths to find teachers who not only will fit into their private community, but who are intellectually curious, sound scholars, and teach with passion and skill.

Public school principals who put teaching first and bus schedules second also maintain that the teachers are the key to a successful school.

Bad Teachers Are Mean, Intellectually Dishonest, Ill-prepared. Good Teachers Are Passionate, Skillful, Intellectually Curious, Scholarly.

There are many mentally cruel teachers in U.S. classrooms; men and women whose prejudices cloud their

48

sense of fair play and numb their academic integrity. Some teachers are subtle in their attempts to destroy the spirit of those they dislike or distrust; others are obvious about the way they treat students of one race, or creed, or socio-economic group, or learning ability.

There are dumb teachers; men and women who are not eager learners, but dullish folks who like to follow patterns and are willing to spend day after day watching students follow patterns, with little enthusiasm and varying degrees of interest and skill.

There are frightened teachers; those who want to hold onto their jobs, as the job means a steady income, albeit less than in almost any other profession requiring comparable college preparation and licensing.

Of course, there are superb and dedicated teachers. They are already doing the job as well as they can; other suggestions in other chapters will help to smooth the way for these reformers. It's not the good teachers who need improving; it's the bad ones.

And right now, and certainly for the remainder of this decade, it's a buyer's market; some one million persons more than there are teacher openings have been certified to teach in U.S. schools.

This means new hirings need not be made blindly or hastily. With less than 100,000 openings annually, and ten times that number available, clearly one way to improve schools is to pick the best from among the qualified.

That's an easy way to improve teaching compared to the problem of trying to improve those already tenured who are ignorant or incompetent or both. There's nothing wrong, per se, with greying faculties; but everything wrong with greying and unteachable faculties.

We'll come back to some suggestions for methods of choosing new teachers, and ways to employ them for the first one or two years so that they learn while doing, and not just "do."

Are there really thousands of "unteachable" teachers holding down jobs in thousands of classrooms coast-to-coast? Or are there just a few unteachables; and a great many who would do better if they were taught to do so?

One thing for certain, the veteran third-grade teacher

who has gone sour (or was never particularly sweet) must not have another 29 third graders handed to him/her in the next school year. The algebra teacher, too, who is not a mathematician must not be allowed to stultify 150–200 students this next school year.

Remove Poor Teachers from Classrooms Immediately.
Let Them, Instead, Do Lunch, Hall, Recess, Phone,
and Supply-Room Duty.

The rotten apples must be taken out of our nation's classrooms.

One way to do this, and it can be done tomorrow without waiting for the end of the school year, is to remove from the classroom all who cannot teach and are themselves unteachable. Double up if you have to, redistribute the pupils, make wider use of strong classroom aides, but reassign these tenured teachers to non-classroom duties.

Have these poor teachers monitor recess and lunch shifts; let them keep the attendance books, organize and supervise bus schedules, distribute materials from the supply room, handle all copying and duplicating chores, answer phones, run all audio-visual equipment. In other words, let them handle the plethora of chores which do not put them in a teaching situation.

You cannot improve your school unless you remove from the classroom the cruel and unteachable. But you can improve the whole atmosphere if you teach the teachers who are teachable to teach. Yes, they should have learned on their own, but really, when the problem of learning to teach is compared with other comparable professional skills, the present system is way off base.

If you were to take banking and currency in college and were to secure an entry-level bank job on graduation, you can be sure that (1) you would not be given a separate department to handle on your own; and (2) neither would you be expected to supervise your own professional growth.

No, your employer would put you under a more experienced person, would carefully monitor your abilities and interests, and would see that you got the proper training as you moved "up" in the bank's structure. Or, if your employer found you were only interested in reaching a specific level of knowledge and ability, you would be kept at that level under supervision for as long as you and your employer were satisfied.

Ah, but school systems hire the neophyte, provide next to no supervision, literally shut the door, assigning near identical duties to the first-year teacher as to the veteran.

And what's worse is that too many schools keep assigning pupils to incompetent (cruel or unteachable) teachers, shut the door to the hall, and figure that those kids will "catch up next year."

And so, one quick way to improve every school in the nation is to keep away from close contact with pupils all teachers who aren't particularly good at their job.

Those who aren't good at what they are doing need to be told that they aren't measuring up; they should be told that they may no longer work directly with pupils until or unless they demonstrate the ability to teach well. If district or state regulations prohibit the dropping of these adults from school district payrolls, then do as is suggested above—give them non-teaching assignments.

What's just been said so simply is not simple at all. The business of determining when a teacher is too poor to be given a classroom assignment is fraught with dangers. So fraught, in fact, that poor teachers have received—year after year—teaching assignments when neither they nor their supervisors and certainly not the assigned pupils wanted those teachers.

Organize So Some Teach and Some Don't.
Pay on a Different Scale. Change the Vacation Allowance.
Expect an Eight-Hour Workday.

The problem is not, as many would insist, one of judging what is more subjective than objective; no, the problem is that schools are not organized around the principle that some adults in the building should be teaching and others should be relieving good and competent teachers of non-teaching duties.

A different organization is called for to accommodate the teacher who shouldn't have been tenured in the first place, or to accommodate the teacher who, for whatever reasons, fails to teach well but is not in any way a candidate for dismissal because of flagrant non-professional activity.

What is also needed, particularly for that community which wants to assure that the best qualified are the ones doing the actual teaching, is a peer review structure which includes the teacher under judgment as part of the process.

Before suggesting ways to handle this very touchy issue, let's return to the teacher who has already been identified (perhaps even self-identified) as poor and who must be removed from the classroom. Even if you are not allowed, through local or state regulations, to compensate these staffers at a rate commensurate with the clerical duties to which you are assigning them, you can—and should—reassign working hours.

Clerks generally work eight-hour days for 48, 49, or 50 weeks a year. It's common knowledge that one reason poor teachers stay in jobs which they aren't good at is the short hours in the working day and the vacations and holidays, which exceed by several weeks what most employed adults are allowed.

By taking away these generous working conditions, enough incentive might be provided so that these poor teachers will resign, and hence help to improve the whole atmosphere of the school. But better the service personnel should be crabby than that children should be taught by the unwilling.

It's the good teacher who needs time away from routine activities to recharge that inner battery of joy and dedication; it's the ones who work directly with pupils and give continuously of themselves as carers and directors who should be sheltered and protected and compensated at higher and higher rates as they gain in understanding and skill. It's these adults who should have more than two or three weeks of vacation time a year and who should get almost the same breaks away from the classroom as the children are given.

But what about those teachers who are poor only because they are untrained; who are not unteachable but untaught?

One way to help the teachable is to assign them to observe other teachers. Even the very best teachers need to do this; need to test a new method against use by an old master in that method. And it's often those teachers one listens to in halls and foyers and dining areas comparing techniques, sharing insights, and stimulating each other.

Let the Poor Watch the Rich. Have Teachers Who Don't Know How, Watch Teachers Who Do.

But the poor teacher—for a host of fairly obvious reasons—doesn't take these opportunities to hone skills. And, once again, most schools are not organized around a need to do something about these poor teachers other than to hold down pay raises, and recommend inservice courses.

Once a week for certainly no less than ten weeks, some administrator in the school should take the class of a poor teacher, freeing the poor teacher to observe a master teacher. After each session, the poor teacher and an administrator should talk over what the master teacher did that was "good," or "special," or "exceptional."

Sometimes the problem with poor teachers is that they've forgotten how to learn. They concentrate too much on organization and too little on what makes connectors for certain children studying certain disciplines.

We've got a national problem—an enormous body of teachers in place in our classrooms who have never taken high school, much less college, physics.

We should now place all elementary school teachers who never took college physics (probably no more than three or four to a given class) in a college-preparatory physics class. Studying along with the students (and with a few peers), getting a handle on those laws which govern matter and energy, learning to apply math principles to practical concerns, sharing in discovery teaching, and alternating teaching with learning should prove to be of enormous benefit to a good teacher and of inestimable benefit to a poor teacher.

There are at least two reasons why poor teachers should take a physics course at the nearest secondary school. The most obvious is the need for all adults in our technological society to understand the interrelationship between energy and matter. The not-so-obvious reason is the need for a poor teacher to be stimulated with a proper sense of intellectual vigor.

A few poor teachers are poor at their jobs because they are selfish, hence they don't care whether all the children under their jurisdiction learn and thrive. Taking a physics course, along with a few other adults and a room full of teenagers, might—or might not—jolt them out of their inward leanings and stimulate an interest in unselfish dedication to even the most "difficult" learners.

And even if poor teachers remained poor, at the very least their teaching would improve, as they would have a clearer understanding of the physical laws underlying space and movement.

No One Should Teach in a U.S. School Who Has Not Taken High School or College Physics.

Those who determine the requirements for certification to teach have never before required college physics of all would-be teachers, be they aiming for the primary level or for the teaching of English composition at the high school level. But it should become a truism throughout all teacher education: No one should teach in a U.S. school who has not taken a good course in physics, particularly a course which requires the understanding of sound mathematical concepts.

Our common schools were designed 80 years ago to meet the needs of a rural agricultural economy; much of our teacher training still echoes this long-past era in American history. We're now rapidly passing out of the industrial age into a period of technological advancement.

Soon our colleges and universities which train teachers will catch up with this development; but until they do, school districts, saddled with older staff teachers, must do some training of their own. What better way than to place in every college-preparatory physics class no less than two and probably no more than five teachers from around the school district.

Again, since the teaching will come during school time, a substitute will need to be found for the teacher's class. This could be an administrator, or even an aide.

Teachers taking physics should not have to be graded on their work, nor compensated on the salary schedule for doing what they should have done as students. This course in physics should be part of the year's assignment—and the purpose should be not only to teach physics to a teacher in a position to pass on his/her new knowledge to pupils, but to rejuvenate each teacher's desire to learn and hence to teach.

If one traces back the school experience of those who are poor teachers, two trends emerge: they avoided the "hard" subjects; they are memorizers. Study after study has revealed that no group of college students had worse scores on qualitative standardized tests than those students choosing to major in education.

What follows is a true incident which took place one day in Princeton, New Jersey, at the Educational Testing Service. I was part of a group of policy board members being shown what happens—along an assembly line—when pre-addressed envelopes are sent in by upcoming test-takers.

The woman in charge pointed to a "reject" pile (relatively small, given the flow of envelopes passing through the hands of about a dozen workers) and explained that they had to be dealt with specially as something was wrong.

To illustrate, she picked up several and showed us that the name was missing in one case, no check in several, insufficient data in another, and so on.

We were looking at a flow of applications to take the Graduate Record Examination, but I was curious about the reject pile and so asked: "You appear to be getting less than 10 percent rejects; is that about standard?"

"Oh my, no; it varies."

This gave rise to my next question: "Does one set of applications have a greater percentage of rejects than all the others?"

She grinned. I would like to note that she gave the impression that she was a smiler, and not a grinner; nevertheless, the grin was unmistakable in response to my question. She looked back over her shoulder, put her hand on my elbow, and said: "The teacher's exam!" And the grin gave way to a giggle which I punctuated with a big laugh.

The women along the assembly line wanted to be let in on the joke; they confirmed the statement. It seems that as many as one in three applications for the teacher exam is incorrectly made out.

Selfishness aside as a reason for one teacher being poor and another competent, the very fact that many students did well in school by memorizing what fairly dull teachers expected them to memorize has perpetuated a really quite unnecessarily low quality of teaching skills.

Memorizers Are Not Condemned to a Life of Memorizing: They Can Learn to Be Problem-Solvers, Creative Thinkers, Conceptualizers.

Memorizers are not condemned to a life of memorizing; they can use that skill to free themselves for creative thinking, for problem solving, for conceptualizing.

It just might be that teachers who themselves used memorizing as their main learning tool, and hence have difficulty thinking of ways to help children learn who are not natural memorizers, might come alive in a well-taught physics class. The stimulation of learning how and why things work might jolt these teachers into thinking of ways to present what they teach so that it's understandable to a wide range of learners.

It's a truism—every good teacher is a good learner; likes to learn, is curious, seeks out those who want to share knowledge and experiences. Is not the opposite true? That a poor teacher is a poor learner, a non-reader, a passive thinker.

A reader might wonder, if I feel a course in physics is so very important, why I do not call for inservice courses in physics. Certainly there must be enough evidence from the Atlantic to the Pacific and from the Rio Grande to the St. Lawrence Seaway that inservice courses taught by the same folks who so poorly prepare undergraduates to be teachers in the first place don't improve schools. Their courses certainly don't improve the teachers who take them.

What teachers got too much of as undergraduates was the notion that teaching is organizing classrooms, assigning pages of examples, correcting assignments from an answer book, and generally acting as traffic cops from classrooms to bathrooms to lunchrooms to the late bus home. The problem with many poor teachers is they think the above is teaching! And furthermore, they were taught this was so by those they had every reason to trust—their college professors.

Of course classrooms must be organized, but more than that, those who teach in them need to know how to teach. And need to know how to teach a variety of learners.

What to do in place of inservice courses?

Yes, if you're not already qualified, take that physics class.

Every Teacher Read a Book a Term—
Discuss It with Scholars, with Other Teachers,
with Concerned Community Members.

But also join with other teachers and perhaps interested community members and read each term a book that explores some important ideas touching on education. You could start with the following pair; they're recommended because they teach us to look outside ourselves and to embrace the world.

Toward the 21st Century: Education for a Changing World, by Edwin O.Reischauer (Knopf), is slim and powerful.

Innocents Abroad, by Mark Twain, is deceptively potent. Twain would have us look at how we look at others, and teach us by so doing to learn how better to reach out to others.

Reischauer explains the theme of his book:

> We need a profound reshaping of education if mankind is to
> survive in the sort of world that is fast evolving. While the
> world is in the process of becoming a single great mass of
> humanity—a global community, as it is sometimes called—
> the very diverse national and cultural groupings that make up
> the world's population retain attitudes and habits more ap-
> propriate to a different technological age, when the contrast-
> ing civilizations existed far removed from one another and the
> well-being of individuals was determined within largely self-
> contained nations, or even smaller communities.

Then he concludes:

> The continuance of such parochial attitudes in an interdepen-
> dent, closely knit world would probably spell catastrophe.
> Basically this is an educational problem.

This is an educational problem, and one which every
teacher should be studying with an eye to helping all children better understand both the roots of parochialism and
the necessity of global interdependence.

It would be money wisely invested if a copy of each of
these books was given to every teacher. Perhaps parent
groups could participate in both reading the same books
and holding seminars to discuss them.

The *Paideia Proposal*, by Mortimer Adler is, of course, a
"must."

Think of the stimulating environment that would be
created in the classroom where the teacher was exploring
these uncharted waters in consort with many of the business and educational leaders in the community.

The next term, all might buy and read Eric W. Johnson's
slim and enormously useful volume *Teaching School: Points
Picked Up*. This master teacher claims his book is "for anyone who is teaching, wants to teach, or knows a teacher."
Any school that had every teacher read and discuss the
many ideas proferred in this book would, I guarantee it,
become a better school.

Mr. Johnson, like Mark Twain, is not without a sense of
humor. He begins the preface: ". . . to me teaching is as

noble, challenging, stimulating, and rewarding a job as one can set one's heart and mind to—except on Fridays and during the month of February."

Which leads to another: "What are the three best reasons to teach school?" Give up? The answer: "June, July, and August."

We're not teaching all the children who come to school how to read. There have been some suggestions that there are "certain" children or "certain family conditions" that make it well nigh impossible for some children to learn to read.

Pedagogists tell us that the only children who cannot be taught to read are those with severe brain damage.

And so, one way to improve schools is first to acknowledge that poor readers are the fault of the school, and second to teach all the teachers how to teach those who don't naturally learn to read on their own.

Let the Teacher Who Knows How to Teach Reading to Those Who Need to Learn Teach the Teachers Who Don't Know How to Teach.

It's a very rare school which doesn't have at least one very, very good reading teacher. It's even rarer to find a school which has made use of this fact to help other teachers learn how to teach reading. It's incredible, but time and again one hears of a teacher who has had enormous success teaching reading working next door to a teacher with a much less successful record, and learns that they have never worked together in a "teacher-pupil" relationship.

I can't believe this would happen if we were talking about an aquatic school and we had one teacher of swimming who was particularly successful and another who was marginal, and where near drownings were of constant concern to the administrators.

You can be sure that the poor swimming teacher would be fired. But let's suppose the aquatic school offered tenure and the poor teacher was not fireable. Then we can assume that every effort would be made by those who knew how to teach swimming to help the one who was failing to teach well.

The failure to read is not as dramatic as the failure to swim; that is, death is unlikely to result from the failure. Yet it is a kind of certain death to live in a literate world and not be literate—particularly if the illiteracy is the result of poor teaching and not of some inner, irradicable problem particular to the learner.

Let me give a specific example of a very good reading teacher and of the failure of the school system to do anything much to have her teach the other primary-grade teachers how to teach reading. And let me give another example where such sharing resulted in enormously improved reading ability throughout an entire school.

We'll call our reading teacher Ms. White. With her second graders she adopted an individualized reading program, using story books (not basal readers) as the texts. When one child finished a book, he or she went over it with Ms. White, proving to her satisfaction that the pupil not only could read the words but got the meanings of the story. Then that pupil was allowed to check out the next pupil who wanted to read that particular book.

In this way, every pupil among the 27 became teachers; and as all research shows, the pupil who tutors another learns the most from the experience.

From time to time Ms. White would ring a little bell on her desk and reveal that something interesting had come up in a book discussion. A homonym, for example, and what appeared to be a "spontaneous" discussion would ensue.

At least once a month each child wrote his or her own book, bound it, did the illustrations, and had it entered into the library of books which could be read.

Often a child who read a book made out a list of important questions which Ms. White would attempt to answer herself, and then, with some editing, permit this list to be part of a "test" of reading ability for all others interested in reading that book.

From time to time children chose a character from one of

the books and told about the character before the whole class; they thought it was a game of who could guess the character first and of who could name the book from which the character came.

Ms. White knew it was yet another way to stimulate beginning readers to "feel" the thoughts behind the words.

I made an informal check on 15 of Ms. White's second graders ten years later. I talked with each graduating senior and at least one of their parents. Oh, yes, most certainly they remembered the second grade. Yes, without prompting, "That's the year I learned to read."

Their position in a very large senior class—all 15 still in the system were in the top 10 percent.

Spend a Half Day Each Week In a Better Teacher's Classroom—Observing, Noting, Participating, Learning.

How many other primary teachers in the system used such an individualized reading method? Almost none. How many other primary teachers in the system knew for certain that some children need to be taught by one method, some by another, and most through a combination of methods? Perhaps only Ms. White.

Had every poor primary teacher in that school system spent one-half day a week in Ms. White's room observing and participating, it is almost certain each would have returned to his/her own classroom much the wiser and much more able to treat each learner as an individual, and not as part of a "reading group."

And since the law holds that the tutor always learns more than the tutee, even Ms. White would have become a better teacher for the opportunity to share as a professional.

The other case features an excellent reading teacher who became the principal of an elementary school. She spent the first few weeks of school sitting in on class after class when reading was being taught. And she discovered, just as any principal would, that some of the teachers were doing a good job, and some fair, and some a very poor job.

She also decided that the classes were too large. How to solve that problem?

Since it was a neighborhood school with only a few of the children coming by bus and a great many driven by parents, she instituted a different arrival and departure schedule.

Make Every Teacher a Reading Teacher. Split the School in Half to Make the Classes Smaller. Tutor the Needy.

All the little boys were to come at 8 A.M., and the full teaching staff was to teach reading to the boys until 9. At 9 the girls arrived and "regular" classes were held until 2 P.M. Then the little boys got out of school "early," and the little girls stayed for an hour; again with all teachers participating in the teaching of reading.

Once a week the principal held a sort of clinic, asking teachers who used one method to share that method with all the others. Often this was done with children actually being taught lessons.

Also, reading groups were formed on the basis of ability and not chronological age. Children who could read well and tested well above grade level were put in larger groups and urged to deepen their understanding of concepts and vocabulary.

Children who were struggling and had one or more reading "blocks" were almost hand taught, and if a teacher was having difficulty, the rule was to share that problem with the other teachers and to get help from all who had something to contribute.

The result, as you might well imagine, was that failure to learn to read was almost eliminated; also, the average reading ability of all age and grade groups improved.

A gym teacher, at first more than a little reluctant to participate, discovered he "had a way with phonics." And child after child got to spend that special hour alone with him "doing" phonics. A treat for both pupil and teacher.

Let's say your school couldn't accommodate two entering and leaving times, yet you wanted to double the number of teachers teaching reading and cut in half the class size.

Obviously, one way would be to engage half the school population in some group activity overseen or supervised by just one or two teachers; or perhaps one teacher and one or two aides. That would free the whole staff to work with half the population on reading.

What could be taught in such massive groups? Why half the school population, early in the morning, could be learning folk songs and dances on the playground or in the gymnasium.

Half the population could listen to someone read a very good story for half an hour and then draw a picture to go with what they heard for the other half.

Half the population could watch a movie or a special television program and then discuss what they had seen and what they thought about it.

Maybe half the population could be learning crafts with a number of community people all organized by the parent-teacher organization. One school I know does this during the noon hour on days when the kids can't go out on the playground.

Older folks in the neighborhood actually wait for cloudy and bad-weather days so they can come over to school and knit, tat, sew, tell stories, listen to stories, or play backgammon, Parchesi, Monopoly, etc., with small groups of children before and after their 20 minutes of eating time.

Teachers Need to Watch Teachers.
Teachers Need to Tutor Teachers.
Teachers Need to Work with Teachers.

But let's get back to the basics in the curriculum. Teachers need to watch teachers; teachers need to tutor teachers; teachers need to work with other teachers. I suppose, as a last resort, some telling might take place. But generally, teachers telling teachers doesn't work; but teachers working together to solve a shared problem works wonders.

And that's particularly true if the one getting the

teachers together understands that the skills natural to one are foreign to others, allowing them to eagerly accept their differences and at the same time drop competition for cooperation.

An enormous amount of research has been done to determine the effects of class size. Naturally, teachers' unions want the ratio to be as low as possible so that more teachers will be hired. Naturally, school board members representing the taxpayers want the sizes to be as large as possible.

Both have undertaken massive studies of the problem, and to the chagrin of National Education Association and American Federation of Teachers organizers, class size—particularly between 25 and 35—appears to make little difference when classes are taught by the group method and classrooms are self-contained.

What is astounding is that most teachers and teacher organizers keep beating that dead horse over and over, talking about the need to lower class size. But the problem, as so much of the research indicates, is not size but teaching methods.

The algebra teacher who uses lecture, drill, and homework, all based on a textbook full of rules and drills, has a very hard time arguing that she would do a better job if there were 26 pupils in her class instead of 29.

The truth of the matter is, algebraic concepts need to be conceptualized almost on an individual basis, pupil by pupil in discussion and problem-solving. One student will easily understand the relationship of negative and positive numbers, while another may need to test out some practical applications before the "light" comes on.

Any math teacher with more than ten pupils has got an uphill climb if she/he doesn't organize for full individualization. One method of going about this is for the algebra teacher to learn to give diagnostic tests, and then, reading the results, tailor the teaching to small group learning styles.

Another, of course, is to make every pupil a teacher. Just as Ms. White did with each storybook for her beginning readers, so can the algebra teacher ask those who grasp one concept to be the tutors for all who do not.

Make Every Pupil a Teacher.
Class Size Then Is One to One,
And Tutor Learns More than Tutee.

Also, the pupils in Algebra II need to tutor, as tutors learn from tutoring and tutees need the individualized attention. It wouldn't be time wasted for Algebra II pupils to spend two periods a week teaching Algebra I pupils; it would, instead, be a gain in learning were this to take place.

Meanwhile, the "regular" algebra teacher, supervising the tutoring, would broaden his/her own skills in how to get algebraic concepts across. And as the teacher's skills improve, so the pupils will meet with more and more success.

Since it's clear that such a circle of teaching and learning would benefit all in that circle, isn't it amazing that so many schools are organized on a linear basis and arguing that there is no possibility of creating a circle of learning? Further, it doesn't cost any more money to create the circle; just more caring about the learner.

Some 50 teachers signed up for a workshop in learning how to teach writing. I spent a day with them. A threatened air-controller strike didn't take place, and since that fact allowed me to be on time to teach the class, I asked that each one write the first 100 words of a newspaper story explaining what had happened.

All knew about the impending strike—all had read about the strike in the local papers; all had heard about it on radio and television.

"Take ten minutes," I said, "and write the first 100 words of your story."

No, they couldn't carry out that assignment to please themselves. Interestingly, while they knew they needed to know more than they did about teaching writing, and hence had signed up for the course, all agreed afterward that they didn't know they couldn't write.

I asked if there were any in the room who could play the French horn. They all said they could not. I asked how they knew they could not, and of course they said it was because they had never done so.

Musicians Practice Scales.
Teachers, too, Should Practice the Basics.

I then asked, since none of them had ever done any professional writing, why they thought they knew how to write. Ah, but . . . yet I then asked about whether they knew any music at all. Whether they played any instrument at all. Whether they had ever sung a note. And so on.

Together we had to agree that the reason these teachers weren't writers was solely because they didn't practice writing skills.

Again, incredible as it may seem, schools are organized in such a way that teachers never have to write. Further, whenever they do, no one edits what they have written. Nor is there a process in place for writing, editing, rewriting, further editing, rewriting, final editing.

Yet, in every newspaper office in the world, the most senior writers, Pulitzer prize winners included, write and rewrite and rewrite and are edited and edited and edited.

Teachers do an enormous amount of talking, and for the most part, reports to parents are either oral or in code. Letter code for about half the schools and number code for the remainder.

The business and civil service world exists on the well-crafted memo. Teachers almost never have to write such missiles as part of their duties and seldom ever teach pupils how to write them.

Let's go to the world of the professional musician— particularly the one who plays for the public in group performances. Hours and hours are devoted to restudying basic principles and techniques so that when the actual piece is performed there will be no ragged edges.

What hours do teachers spend practicing and drilling on those 3 Rs we're all so fond of demanding children learn?

If you learn that Rudolf Serkin spends up to three hours a day practicing scales and other basics of piano playing, you think how very fine and recognize that genius of expression is built on hours and hours of good hard labor.

If you asked all the teachers in a school system to devote

at least an hour a day to practicing some of the basic skills to hone them for the performances they will give in their classrooms, they would look at you with astonishment and, be assured, tell you it's not in their contract.

But isn't it?

First Write—Then Rewrite. Next: Ask an Editor to Suggest Changes. And Next, Rewrite.

Let's review five types of writing. First, description. Perhaps for the first two months of the school year each teacher could be asked to write a description of a methods class he'd taken in college. Pair the teachers, asking that they exchange papers after the first draft, expecting the other person in the pair to do a thorough editing job.

A rewrite would then be in order, and each teacher would be given another partner. Again, each would edit the work of the other.

Halfway through the period, a group of teachers would present some well-written descriptions found in current literature; small-group discussions would be held, noting how those in print had solved a problem the teachers were having with their writing.

Repeat the writing assignment, staying with the same topic, but demanding that the reader be assailed by feeling, seeing, hearing what the writer is writing. Spend up to a month of class sessions with writing homework.

Now move to writing based on contrasts and comparisons. Again call for pairing, with all writers becoming editors, and this time request that every teacher bring to a small-group discussion a professional's work exemplifying the very best of comparison writing.

Keep up this pattern of writing, editing, and finding sterling examples of the craft in professional works through analytical writing, criticism, and finally snythesis.

Should a teacher who did this in 1984–1985 have to do it all over again in 1985–1986? Does Serkin have to practice scales and chords? Does the professional baseball player have to practice batting? Surely after 12 seasons in the majors, following at least 8 years of varsity play in school and college, the pro doesn't need to practice "that" fundamental all over again. Of course he does.

It really is quite impossible to improve the teaching of writing in U.S. schools unless the teachers themselves write and write and write.

More Socratic Teaching Needed.
Less Didactic Teaching Needed.
Lecturing on How Not to Lecture—Out.

An enormous mistake was made when "new" math was all the rage. Those college professors who were so willing to come teach in the lower grades and to show what could be done if the teaching was conceptual and creative, were then asked to teach teachers how to do the same.

Their colossal blunder? They lectured about how to teach by the Socratic method!

The teachers who didn't know how to conceptualize had, of course, as students been visual learners and memorizers. And here were these gurus who used the Socratic method with enormous precision and intuition with little children falling back on their higher education robes to lecture. Hence, the college professors reinforced the teachers' own memorization habits and wreaked havoc with their later attempts to let children "discover" the rules of algebra.

Teachers who aren't naturally curious and eager discoverers, who don't relish trying new ways to think through old concepts, won't change their ways through lectures which tell them not to lecture.

The solution? Let those who love the Socratic method teach other teachers by the Socratic method. Just as teachers must read to be good teachers of reading; and just as they must write to be good teachers of writing; so they should do math to be good math and arithmetic teachers.

Again, once a week let those who falter in the teaching of arithmetic and math visit the class of a master math teacher and observe, help out, try out, think about, and finally comprehend the meaning behind the arithmetic statements or processes.

Let the Teacher of a Second Language
Talk with the Speaker of a Second Language;
In Fact, Insist that this Occur.

If you want to improve the teaching of foreign languages in your schools, then pair each teacher with a native speaker of the language she/he teaches. The time was when it was considered "enough" for language teachers to follow a text and provide lessons and explanations in English regardless of the language being learned. That's no longer considered a good standard; French teachers should speak French and Russian teachers Russian.

Perhaps there are enough native speakers on the school faculty to talk and share language teaching ideas with each teacher; but more often it will be necessary to reach out into the community to get the kind of practice so important for a sound accent and a deep cultural understanding behind word definitions.

Why not start a French-only lunch table to which community French speakers are invited, and include not only teachers but a few pupils?

To Teach by a Different Method,
the Teacher Must Learn by that Method.

Once I offered any pupil in grade six, in a very large elementary school, the opportunity to do some informal math once a week in the cafeteria before the lunch hour began.

Anyone could come who wanted to; no homework, but everyone at the session must participate.

The room was filled to overflowing with eager math puzzlers. "Base 5," I would call out and follow with "count off." The response would begin: "One, two, three, four, one oh, one one, one two, one three, one four, two oh. . . ." If you gave an incorrect number, you had to stand up. You could only sit down again if you got the next problem correct.

And the next might have been: "If ¼ of 20 is not 5 but 4, then what should be ⅓ of 10?"

Or: "Add 8 to a certain number, subtract 8 from the sum, multiply the remainder by 8, and dividing the product by 8 you'll get 4. What is that 'certain number'?"

Week after week all teachers were invited to join us; week after week none of them came. Then an edict to all elementary teachers—they must take an inservice course in how to teach "new" math. To that they came, listened to the lectures, and learned little either about how to teach informal math or how to think mathematically.

Since each week's lesson in the cafeteria started with drills on basics in the most creative ways possible—often, after the first few weeks, thought up and run by the pupils—the one missing element was the faculty. Yes, time should have been arranged for every elementary teacher to sit in on those informal sessions on a regular basis— they, too, having to stand until they could get the answers correct.

Another way to help teachers out is to pair them up. Or, better said, let them choose a partner for a year with the idea that each has something to teach the other, but that one is more the master teacher and the other has much to learn.

For many teachers, it will just be finding out about more and more methods; for others the need will be both to learn more substance for what they teach and to discover new ways to put ideas across. Develop a kind of school buddy system, expecting, of course, that all new teachers be paired with the most masterful of teachers, and that during some years master teachers might have the opportunity to buddy with another master teacher.

The "Buddy" System Used by Swimming Teachers Prevents Many Drownings. A "Buddy" System Pairing Strong Teachers with Weak Could Prevent Many Failures.

Perhaps they might try some team teaching, but that's not the purpose I see for the pairing. Instead, I see professional courtesy and understanding; a kind of sharing of ideas; a concern that pupils not fail because we as teachers have failed.

What about improving the 100,000 new teachers out of the million or so with certificates who start new teaching jobs each year? I turn for help to the private sector, where little Shady Hill School in Cambridge, Massachusetts, pioneered an internship for highly selected teacher candidates.

Shady Hill, to oversimplify, uses the core curriculum at the elementary level, and has done so from its founding years ago. This made the school doubt the ability of those just entering the teaching profession; doubt, that is, that they would understand the methods used at Shady Hill. At the same time, they wanted to attract sound scholars, committed young people.

They offered a first-year internship to graduates with outstanding college records. Yes, the neophytes were not only paired with master teachers, but watched over by all teaching staff.

And the neophytes, knowing they were interning, looked for ways to better what their elders were doing as well as to learn the how behind the why.

There would appear to be no reason on this earth for public school districts to take graduates right out of college, no matter what colleges claim for their four or five years of study, and place them in full charge of a class or a course.

The First-Year or Beginning Teacher Should Not Be Given a Full Teaching Load; Instead, Should Join the Staff for a One- or Two-Year Training Period, Be Paired with a Mentor, and Supervised as an Intern.

Conversely, there would seem to be every reason to hire all beginning teachers as interns; to provide them with part-time teaching assignments, to pair them with a master, and to provide them with a range of experiences so that they may find that area of teaching for which they are either best suited or that most interests them.

By placing new teachers in teams, a school not only provides a better learning environment for the pupils but for all the teachers as well. It's quite possible that the first-year intern will have learned skills in college that the older teachers have only read about. While new teachers teach new "tricks," the older teachers can teach them their "old tricks."

Once a school or school district is satisfied with a new teacher (the second or third year), it should not offer tenure, but a multiple-year contract of up to five years.

Tenure came into being in the U.S. during the Great Depression. Tenure was a way for two-year normal school graduates to keep from having to compete for jobs with those four-year college graduates whose professional jobs had disappeared.

Not Tenure, but Multiple-Year Contracts. Expect Teachers, Coaches, and Administrators to Have to Qualify—Then Requalify—for the Positions They Occupy.

This, too, was the motivation behind certification requirements. Thousands of bankers, for example, were out of work; they all were skilled in basic math, many also in bookkeeping skills. They could well have staffed all math classes.

The schools, on the other hand, were staffed in math and business courses by those who had earned only two-year degrees and were vulnerable due to the fact that half or more of the courses they had taken were methods courses in how to organize business classes. Most of those teachers had never had business careers; had only gone to school and then started teaching.

During the Depression a few professional men and women invested the necessary time and money to take whatever courses were necessary to earn the required certification and squeezed their way into the schools through the attrition route, since tenure was clogging the entries.

In the 1960s one could still find some of these marvelous teachers who stayed on in the schools long after they could have returned to the profession they had been in before the Depression. They are all gone now; with few exceptions all schools—public and private—are filled with teachers whose undergraduate years were spent meeting teacher certification requirements.

It is no wonder, then, that so many of the teachers already in place in U.S. schools need improving; and, further, no wonder that many of them don't know that they need improving.

Without being put in a situation where your teaching can be compared to another's, it's often well nigh impossible to understand why your results are not as good as those of some other teacher.

Too often a teacher who knows two or three methods decides that all learners fit into one of two or three types. The teacher who knows four or five methods generally recognizes that he/she has only got hold of the tip of the iceberg and that there are probably as many ways to teach children as there are children.

Also, some teachers may easily use puppetry for teaching; another may find a way through music; yet another through role playing; and yet another through a deep sense of caring. And this caring translates into "tricks." Let me cite an example.

Old Teacher Can, too, Be Taught New Tricks.

I had been sent to a first-grade room, assured by the principal that "you'll see the best teaching you've ever seen." The teacher was tiny, not much bigger than her first graders. And she was a bundle of energy, darting about the room like a hummingbird dispensing a little honey on each little group she touched.

Just as I was about to think that the principal was mistaking charm and charisma for teaching, she darted into the closet and out again with a cookie tray full of sand. At a small table three children were waiting for this "treat."

I recognized immediately that she had solved a problem with which I had wrestled long and hard. You see, many children learn by actually touching and feeling, and writing in sand is not only good for their sense of feeling, but with the lightest touch any mistake can be instantaneously erased. This not only helps to build confidence, but eliminates dwelling on incorrect letter formations, spelling, and other tactile errors.

The little teacher had put felt pads on the bottom of the sheet to make it easier to swish when she wanted to erase and start again.

Deftly she urged a youngster to put a word in the sand with his finger. He got the first letter of "dog," the second, and then fumbled for the third.

Swiftly the sand was shaken; the "mistake" disappeared. No trace of it; no memory of it; no reason to fear the consequences of asking a critic what was wrong. Now, in the sand the teacher wrote "d-o-g." She urged her young Aristotle to study it for a moment, then shook the low-sided sheet and invited him to write the word again.

Have You Used a Cookie Tray Full of Sand to Teach Reading and Writing?

Ah! Success! And I guessed what his reward would be—he got to draw a dog in the sand.

The moment that was done, she shook the tray, returned it to the closet, sent the same lad to a bookshelf for an encyclopedia, asked another lad to help him find the section on dogs, and then invited the helper to read part of the material about a certain breed to the one who needed the sandy experience.

That principal was right. She was by far one of the best teachers I had ever seen. But there was one enormous problem with her and with her principal.

She was the best kept secret in a very large school district with a large migrant population of first graders finding it extremely difficult to learn to read English.

To her knowledge—and I could find no others—not one other teacher in the school system, much less in her building, had a cookie tray filled with sand. Yet statistics would tell us that in every group of twenty pupils at least two, and as many as five, could learn better if they could feel what they were seeing and saying.

Many teachers in the system knew about her; most knew her results were "fantastic." Yet no teacher had ever been assigned to work with her on a regular weekly basis; she'd been paired with no neophyte. Her "tricks" were not teachers' room talk.

A good many primary-level teachers, who really want to do a better job, often wonder why it is that they can teach some children to read and not others.

More often than not, the fault lies within the teacher's own style of learning. The teacher with the near photographic memory expects pupils to learn from visual cues and clues. Time and again such a teacher will point to a word or letter or phrase and wonder why so many of the pupils don't "pay attention" or "concentrate." They think the problem is discipline, and a round robin of "Look, look," is followed by "Stay in during recess and copy those words."

The pupil who doesn't naturally look to learn is frustrated, then punished, then forced to repeat a drill which goes against his very means of learning. Copying is a seeing, not a kinesthetic, drill.

Some Learn by Hearing and Repeating. Some by Seeing and Visualizing. Many by Feeling, Touching, Trying.

The aural/oral teacher tends to spell or sound out words. For pupils who seem slow, the teacher speaks LOUDLY and DISTINCTLY. Oh, what a burden this is for the visual learner and how impossible for the kinesthetic learner.

We all use our eyes to learn; we all use our ears to learn; we all need to "try it ourselves" to learn. But each of us uses one way more than another and we all need to combine the three.

It's the rare teacher who knows that writing in sand is essential for one type of learner and would slow down another. And even rarer to find a teacher who knows how to diagnose how children learn.

Which leads to another way to improve our schools. We must use diagnostic tests; we must find out not what a child has already learned, but what it is he/she has not learned, and a hint of the reason why.

Unfortunately, most of what teachers are taught about designing (and analyzing) tests has to do with the collection of learned skills, and not with the writing of items for diagnostic purposes.

The spelling tests given on standardized exams, for example, cannot be used for diagnostic purposes as they do not have an orthographic base. Instead, like many spelling curriculum materials, they are based on common words in use at specific grade levels, and tests are predicated on proofreading skills more than on the knowledge of how a word is built to carry a meaning.

School districts which include or are near major colleges or universities will need to turn to the psychometricians on the campuses to help with a study of diagnostic testing. One marvelous way, of course, is to test the teachers first, then, with their cooperation, analyze the results so that the teachers learn not only what makes up a diagnostic test, but what one does with its results.

Returning to the example, again, of a swimming school. The better swimming teachers know how to give diagnostic tests; it is a matter of life and death for them to know what the beginning swimmer is doing wrong and how each swimmer needs to make it right.

Asking a child to do a "dead man's float" is not assigned solely for the purpose of wanting a child to float in that manner. No, that's a diagnostic test. If the young swimmer rolls into that ball with ease and security, the swimming teacher now knows he or she can go ahead with teaching underwater swimming, the front crawl, the butterfly, and so forth.

Teachers Should Learn How to Give as Well as Read and Interpret Diagnostic Tests; Then Fit the Teaching to the Needs.

A hesitancy, a floundering, an attempt to take the position, but to keep the head out of the water—all are watched with a keen eye by the swimming teacher. What does that little one need to get over that fear or lack of coordination or disorientation or . . .?

The same teaching skills must be applied to reading, writing, and arithmetic. The same kind of attention to detail; the same dedication to recognizing that when the pupil doesn't learn, it's the teacher's job not only to find out why, but to think of some way to teach so that the rough patch is smoothed over.

Let us get back to the beginning teacher. Let's look at some ways to improve schools by improving the intake of teachers. Remember, it is a buyer's market—with the exception, perhaps, of math and science teaching at the secondary level. There the scarcity is acute enough to call for innovative measures to correct.

A young friend of mine went first to a liberal arts college and then to a state college specializing in teacher training and earned a master's degree. He wanted, he thought, to be a history teacher. and he wanted to teach in a "good" school system.

He asked me which one of the suburbs surrounding a large Eastern city had a good reputation. I told him one, and indicated I thought they might not want to hire him. "Why not?" he asked. I was gentle in my answer: "They might not think you scholarly enough." He looked puzzled and said again that he had passed all certification requirements and had an M.A. It was a "what more could you ask for" look which he took out to the school district with him.

He was back the next day. It seems that the personnel department had sent him to the head of the history department and that "this woman" had asked him to name ten history books he had in his own personal library. Learning he had none but some leftover college texts, she dismissed him, indicating it "wasn't worth her time to interview him further."

We talked. I asked why he wanted to teach history if he didn't like it well enough to read it and to keep up with the latest scholarly journals. He said my standards were "unrealistic." That what was needed in junior and senior high schools was someone who could present the textbook material interestingly and keep order in the classroom.

I mentioned a suburb which never had had a reputation

for excellence or innovation. He went there that day and called me from the nearest pay phone after the interview. No one there asked him about his library of history books or what he knew about history or what methods he expected to use to teach history. They looked, instead, at his paper credentials, hired him on the spot, and were delighted to find he was willing to coach a varsity sport.

He's still there. He got tenure the third year. He's not added to his history library; he no longer coaches at school but takes private pupils in that sport, making, as he explains it, "twice as much with half the hassle."

Even a Lousy Teacher Can Be Improved.

He's not mean. He isn't sour. He's not mentally cruel. He is, though, a lousy junior high teacher. He's 40 years old, and has paid off all but two years of the mortgage on his home. How to improve him, and the thousands just like him?

Get him out of a self-contained classroom as soon as possible. Move him up to the high school and require that he teach, with at least two other teachers, a course in the history surrounding the Civil War period which combines English, art/music, and history credits, or some other team-taught, multi-disciplinary, subject-oriented history course.

Require that the team of teachers responsible for this multiple-credit course either stay for three weeks after school lets out, or return three weeks before school begins in the fall. Put the English or the art/music teacher in charge of the team, and require that all work together to build a syllabus.

Locate a nearby Civil War scholar and, with a modest consultant fee, ask him or her to go over the history lessons chosen by the teacher who needs all this help. Insist when school starts that at least two of the team's teachers sit in on all class sessions when they aren't actually doing the teaching.

Or, if this teacher is expected to teach European or Asian history, then team him up with a master teacher and shorten his class assignments by one, assigning him to a language class as a student. (Of course, if he hasn't had physics in college, and most history majors have not, then first assign him to take the high school physics course.) Have this teacher study French, or Spanish, or German, or Italian, or Russian, or Chinese, or . . .

Perhaps the team teaching could be done with a master teacher of a European language and the history teacher. All students taking this course would have to be enrolled in both the language and the history courses, and understand that some of the teaching will be done in the second language.

Our 40-year-old lousy history teacher either will rise to the occasion, and through a combination of his own improved learning and teaching skills provide capable teaching for his pupils, or he will so badly expose his ineptitude that the school administration will have no choice but to remove him from the classroom, giving him clerking and teacher-aide duties for the remainder of his time as an employee of the school district.

Another way to arouse latent scholarly abilities and a desire to be a good teacher would be to assign this teacher to just one history course at the high school which would be monitored by one or more administrators both for content and for the use of good teaching methods. The rest of the school day this teacher would be assigned as a teacher's aide in the classroom of a master teacher—one with a particularly full bag of teaching "tricks." This assignment might even be in a nearby elementary school, with an eye to discovering if the junior high level is perhaps the wrong one for this teacher; and with a further eye to determining if he is teachable, particularly in the area of how to teach.

Reward the Exceptional. Thank the Traditional. Remove the Unteachable.

The next recommendation is hardly new; furthermore it has had very rough going whenever suggested. Yet reason would certainly dictate that this lousy 40-year-old history teacher should not receive the same salary as the highly skilled, excellent teacher with the same academic preparation and years of service.

Today, in most business offices, a supervisor is given a total percent annually by which he may raise his salary budget—say 8 percent. The wise supervisor may explain to some workers that they just do not deserve and hence will not receive any raise at all; to others he will say that they have only proven themselves at a perfunctory level and hence deserve only a 5 percent raise; and to those few who have extended themselves he may be able to award pay raises of 10 or even 12 percent.

If, year after year, the same teachers "go the extra mile," in ten years their salaries might be as much as double that of the teacher who hasn't extended himself at all—has merely done the minimum. Of course, without tenure to keep such a person in place, at the end of the contract period could come the opportunity to replace such a one from the large pool of those more eager to teach and grow.

Of course, there must be safeguards in such salary flexibility involving merit raises and demerit lack of raises. Certainly the teachers involved should be allowed a peer review of the course and arbitration of the amount in question, carried out by others and not the supervisor who made the first decision.

Perhaps enough has been said about how to improve teachers and teaching, and it's time to put the principals under the spotlight.

In the fall of 1982, I was asked to provide the luncheon address for teachers from school districts throughout the state of Vermont who had been singled out locally by their principals as "Outstanding Teachers." It's a day of honor which is a gift from the University of Vermont, and as such, carries with it dignity, honor, prestige, and a moment—for those teachers—when they are somewhat uncomfortably out of their familiar classrooms, receiving the recognition they deserve.

The University of Vermont asks that each teacher be accompanied by the school principal and a school board member if possible. During my remarks I noted that had the awards ceremony required that teachers nominate their principals, and that further they accompany them to the university for a day of celebration, that we probably would have been able to meet in a small elevator and not, as we were, in a large dining hall. But that's better discussed in Chapter Three.

Checklist

1. *Incompetent teachers:* Assign to nonteaching duties.
2. *Weak teachers:* (a) observe strong teachers; (b) team teach with exceptional teachers; (c) choose a master teacher as a mentor.
3. *Unscientific teachers:* Place every teacher who did not take a physics course while an undergraduate in an advanced placement high school physics class.
4. *Unread teachers:* Give every teacher who has not read them copies of these three books and hold public discussions on the implications for schooling: *Innocents Abroad,* by Mark Twain; *Toward the 21st Century: Education for a Changing World,* by Edwin O. Reischauer; *The Paideia Proposal,* by Mortimer Adler.
5. *Unlettered teachers:* Expect all teachers to spend several hours each week writing; to have what they have written edited; to rewrite; be reedited; to rewrite again.
6. *Didactic teachers:* Coach these teachers in how to coach.
7. *Neophyte teachers:* Hire all first year inexperienced teachers as interns; provide each with a mentor.
8. *Testing teachers:* Teach all teachers how to construct and profitably use diagnostic tests to improve the way they teach.
9. *Tenured teachers:* Replace tenure with multiple-year contracts.

Principals: You're once again (or still) under the gun. The taxpayers want better quality schools, and they are pretty sure the problem lies, primarily, with those who do the teaching. The first five items in this checklist can't take place unless you see that they do. Teachers need all the help they can get and the logical place to start is with you—the principal.

Parents: You, too, have a part to play, particularly since school personnel have been trying to argue that it's pupils and not the schools which are responsible for failures. Yet, much of the problem rightfully belongs at the door of the school. You must make sure to support every single teacher who's trying to improve, and make equally sure that not only your child, but every other child in the district, be spared a seriously poor teacher.

School board members and trustees: If the teachers in the district are weak or poor, it's your fault. If you have no merit pay plan in place, it's your fault. If you're treating new teachers as though they were experienced, and they fail their pupils trying to be what they are not, it's your fault. If teachers who are mean are still in self-contained classrooms, it's your fault. And when the teachers and the teaching improve—take much of the credit. You'll deserve it!

Teachers: Don't get your backs up when reviewing this checklist. Don't argue that no one, especially those who write about schools and don't teach in them, knows how difficult your job is. We know it's a very difficult job, and you do deserve a lot more respect and salary than you probably will ever receive. But no one is forcing you to continue teaching, and the children you teach deserve to have you meet the challenges in this checklist to be sure you qualify for the job you're holding. They deserve the best.

Chapter Three
Improving Principals

When I pulled into the visitor's parking area outside a large high school, so did a big panel truck. I was there to meet with some math teachers; the driver of the van was scheduled to give a presentation to ninth graders in the auditorium. That's all we discovered about each other as we headed for the principal's office to sign in.

We met, somewhat to our amusement, at the same breakfast counter in another city the next morning. We talked shop.

It seems he went from school to school sharing slides or movies and giving a lecture about space travel. I was part of a new math group, and I travelled around the United States giving demonstration lessons to interested (and not-so-interested) teachers.

I challenged the space man: Can you tell what the principal of a school is going to be like by what you see, hear, and feel between where you park your car and the principal's office?

His answer was quick and surrounded by a big laugh: "You bet I can!"

"Take yesterday's high school," he continued, "I didn't have any idea when we met in the parking lot whether the principal was male or female. But I could tell from the graffiti on the walls and the litter on the playground that I wasn't going to ask to have the auditorium lights dimmed. I knew I better use the overhead projector, keep crowd control through eye contact, and that I'd only do half the program."

I asked what he had noticed in the halls.

"Oh," he exclaimed, "weren't they awful. Painted what I call puke green; no art work, and every classroom door was closed."

That's where I broke in, "Oh, that's what always gives me a clue about the kind of school—whether those teachers' doors are closed or open; whether there is some sort of 'thing' about quiet in the halls."

I told him about visiting a "pricey" suburban junior high where the guidance counselor took me out into a very silent hall while classes were meeting, asking: "Do you want to hear a very unhealthy sound? Listen." Then he asked: "What do you hear?" I confessed that the building was nearly silent.

There were tears in his eyes, "I know, I know. That's why I'm leaving. I cannot stay where there is no joy. If the 750 children in this building were learning anything at all that was worthwhile you would, at the very least, hear a hum—yet you hear nothing."

I was particularly interested in my breakfast companion's thoughts about school principals. He was not a teacher, nor a former teacher. He was a businessman; a salesman, if you will, of space travel.

He claimed that not only could he tell the type of principal in that short walk from parking lot to office, but that he knew, as well, whether the principal came out of a solid academic background or athletics.

We agreed that we seldom ever found a school building that wasn't home to at least one superb teacher; and further agreed that it was rare to come on a principal we would dare to call "superb." And yet we were in complete agreement that it's the principal who sets the tone for the school.

Not only does the principal set the efficiency/orderliness climate, but he or she establishes the academic intensity. The principal sets the athletic tone, as well. And these administrators are the guardians for the amount of serious art, music, dance, drama, and poetry which abound or are absent from their buildings.

We agreed that it would be well nigh impossible to improve a school and ignore the principal; further, that one had but two choices; to improve or to replace a bad principal.

Replacing a principal is easy—the position isn't tenured. Improving principals, though, is certainly a more humane activity, but it requires not only the cooperation of the principal, but of faculty, staff, students, and parents.

Principals as Students

Starting with the assumption that most school principals played on varsity athletic teams in high school and/or in college, and further that their liberal arts backgrounds are sketchy, and that their graduate work has been in education administration, the need is for most principals to start studying in depth in some basic academic field. For example, a foreign language.

It's the very rare community which does not have someone who is a native speaker of a language other than English. Let each principal find such a person fluent in a language foreign to the principal.

Then let the principal work in a tutorial arrangement with one or more people fluent in the language chosen; let them help direct the principal's reading in the appropriate literature. Using the human resources at hand and available from a local college or university, the principal could explore some of the art, music, dance, drama—yes, the cultural history of the peoples for whom this language is native.

If the chosen language is taught in the school district, then let the principal—just as all teachers in the district sign up for physics classes—enroll in a language class. Enroll, perhaps, as a teacher's aide; or even as "just another" pupil.

There are several facets to improvement in this suggestion. There is the obvious one that at least one community member would be involved in school improvement. Another obvious one is that the principal would be enlarging his/her borders of interest in world and cultural affairs.

Another obvious improvement would be the awakening to a whole new world of literature; another dimension to art history; another people understood from a different perspective.

Of course, the principal would want to join the teachers reading Reischauer's *Toward the 21st Century.*

A less obvious improvement is the opportunity for such a principal to treat school issues as a learning scholar; not as a punitive coach. Perhaps the inclination was there, but all those years of using competition instead of cooperation to determine relationships—particularly between adults and kids—may have smothered the scholarship. A re-kindling of academic interest, particularly in a skill at once practical as well as liberating, should induce a principal to encourage scholarship among teachers and pupils.

Should the principal already be fluent in a second language, then perhaps the need is for study of music. If not instrumental, then choral; if not choral, then appreciation. Again, each principal should look for at least one community member whose love and understanding of music can be shared.

But let us posit that there are principals fluent in a second language and skilled in music to the pre-professional level. Let math and the natural sciences step in for these school administrators. Let them find those in the community whose love of geometry or calculus or symbolic logic is penetrating as well as beautifying. Possibly such a principal could, with the aid of a scientific expert, set up a course of study or a specific academic project, and throughout a school year work away at it, exploring corners in academia where the dust (for that principal) has been thick.

A few statistics are in order. The National Association of Secondary School Principals did a study in 1977 which showed that the undergraduate major of some 27 percent of all principals had been in the social sciences; that 17 percent had majored in physical education; and only 12 percent in the humanities.

At the graduate level, in 1977, the statistic for the humanities was even lower—only 4 percent.

Principals as Readers

If our schools' leaders were to immerse themselves in serious study of the humanities, they would improve our schools by improving themselves.

The principal who has not read and studied widely and deeply in history should either begin an individual history program, or begin taking some demanding courses from sound history scholars as soon as possible.

Of course, an easy first step is to locate some historians in the local community, agree to a reading/discussion program with one or more similarly minded scholars, and begin wrestling with some of the more important ethical and moral decisions facing us all today.

Another quick improvement, for principals as well as selected students, and with carry-over to all staff, would be for principals to read aloud a little each day to an appreciative audience from some thoughtfully chosen text.

What a wonderful tone that would set for any school, for all the students to recognize how important are the deeper thoughts of the finest thinkers to the man or woman in charge of the school; what a marvelous way for students who might otherwise have no opportunity to explore those ideas to be read to by the principal.

I met a principal in an elementary school in the south of England who went round the school in mid morning looking for the child who could well benefit from coming into her office for 15 minutes to listen to her read either poems or portions of plays.

I asked to sit in, and got in for a scene from Shakespeare's *Midsummer Night's Dream*. With what rapture the child listened; and with what conviction the principal read the parts. I falsely assumed that this principal had read and studied Shakespeare in college or university, only to learn she'd not been to university, but had had, due to a corrected illness, a shortened secondary schooling, and was now making up for that lost time. She'd found an English scholar among the parents and one evening a week joined with others in a play reading/discussion group.

I remember, too, talking with the president of a predominantly black college who explained to me that she read aloud during the evening meal five days a week. She read, she explained, from the finest classical literature. Then she confessed, "When I started, I was really a bit selfish. You see, I had never read those classics, and I knew I needed to or I wasn't worthy to direct the academics of the students."

But one of the greatest strengths of many principals is often falsely seen as a weakness—and that is this background in athletics and physical education. Many a strong principal was (and maybe still is) a good coach. One of the quickest improvements all teachers can make is to stop talking (telling and discoursing in the classroom), and to start doing more academic coaching.

Certainly principals who know a great deal about coaching can lead the way for the whole school. No soccer coach worth his cleats would have students day after day play full games, and ignore any footwork drills. Yet, many an English teacher assigns new pages to be read or new themes to be written—sometimes going weeks before drilling on basic reading and writing skills. No, the good English coach—just as the good soccer coach—varies drill and strategy sessions; varies tempo and pitch; varies directions, sometimes lambasting and other times cajoling—saving praise for dessert.

A good junior or senior high school is full of just such coaching in all academic classes. As a music teacher insists that a phrase be played over and over and over again, so the English teacher should ask for a paragraph to be polished, and polished, and polished.

Let all those principals who majored in physical education or who coached a sport direct the teaching staff in coaching skills. There are times to talk to a whole team at once; other times to meet each athlete individually. Good schools run on the same combination—the whole-school address from the principal, and the private heart-to-heart session between one student and the principal.

Principals as Leaders

I asked the crossing guard at a busy school intersection in a large Northern city if the principal of the school was a good one. "Nope," she said instantly and very matter-of-factly. My face formed a question mark, and she looked me in the eye and announced: "She's a bully."

Another city, another crossing guard, about the same size elementary school (1,000 pupils). Same question. Different answer. "So-so. Neither smart nor dumb." What are his best qualities was my next question. A long pause, "He's tidy, but then I think he's priggish." Another long pause. "You know, that's not good for little boys."

I thought to myself that it wasn't good for little girls either. Bully or sissy, neither belong as head or principal of a school.

Teachers, when asked what makes a good principal, talk about getting help with their teaching—someone on the academic cutting edge leading the way.

Custodians, when asked what makes a good principal, talk about the tone and feel of the school and whether all staff are treated fairly. Like the students, they want neither bully nor sissy, neither mean nor disinterested, neither sour nor silly as leadership.

Parents, when asked what makes a good principal, talk about discipline and orderliness and want the athletics as well as the academics to be as good as or better than in the neighboring schools.

Much of what many principals now do regarding the building they control should more properly be done by an administrative assistant or a fiscal officer.

Curiously, this person known as a principal with advanced academic degrees is more often than not expected to oversee bus routes, direct a custodial staff, design playgrounds and athletic fields, handle a line-item budget, put out some sort of bulletin or newsletter to keep parents informed of school activities, manage a cafeteria, and oversee purchasing and distribution of a complicated set of supplies.

Nothing in the paragraph above talks about teaching or

counseling, yet that's really what a good school principal is all about.

The principal who turns over all housekeeping chores, bookkeeping and purchasing, and most of the scheduling of activities to hourly-wage employees in order to free himself or herself to teach and to counsel is an improved principal running an improved school.

In Chapter Two, "Improving Teachers," it was suggested that those who should not any longer be in the classroom be given non-teaching duties. Here are those duties, and many teachers do, in fact, have the skills to direct a kitchen staff even though they don't seem able to teach English or math or history patiently and skillfully to troubled pupils.

The principal who is more storeroom organizer than academic leader, should stick with his storeroom and appoint a head teacher to do what he or she is not qualified to do. That, of course, is the mark of good principals—knowing themselves—understanding their own strengths and weaknesses.

Principals need to lead from strength, but they need before they do that to learn what the strength is in the school they administer. And this brings principals into the area of research. It also moves principals from line-item budgets to program budgeting.

The old line budget showed principals how much of the total went for salaries, wages, and fringe benefits; how much for equipment; how much for operating costs; how much for maintenance and repair. A program budget shows principals what percent of each of those goes into the teaching of foreign languages; how much to fielding a boys' basketball team; how much to advanced-placement calculus, and so forth.

The good principal isn't satisfied with a line-item budget. She/he wants to be able to connect costs to tasks. It takes a little sophistication, but every principal of every school should know what each classroom hour is costing.

This improvement is going to come more and more into

focus as citizens demand merit pay for particularly good teachers.

This raises the whole notion of connecting cost with quality. When principals know program costs, they can make better (and more informed) decisions than they can if they operate out of ignorance. And if quality is the driving force, then improved program budgeting has to be directly related to improved principals and hence to improved schools.

Academic research follows a bit of the same pattern. We know, for example, that time on task is one key to academic success. What then is the time devoted by a student with an indentifiable learning problem to learning how to read? That is, how much for individual practice? How much under professional direction? How much overseen by peers? How much by interested adults?

Another fact we've learned from research is that students with low self-esteem do poorly, have trouble concentrating, are unresponsive to teachers, and fall nearly 100 percent below "average" test levels.

Principals as Counselors

The improved principal knows how to test for self-esteem, how to recognize the danger signs in pupils and teachers, is capable of rearranging schedules and interactions among students to change self-perception for students with something bothering them.

But let's go back to merit pay for a moment. Principals, as well as teachers, need to be paid salaries which are related to the quality of their work. Means must be found to neutralize personality conflicts and outright prejudice. Whatever system is used to determine what is meritorius service and what is not, should be by mutual agreement— between teachers and a principal, and between principals and a superintendent.

We would go a long way toward improving schools— and toward providing more money for our schools—if we thought that the people we were paying weren't just getting more and more money for seniority (or even for courses taken), but were being paid on a scale directly connected to the quality of their work. But, let's get back to the students.

In growing teens, there is a time when physical change is so constant and so compelling that extra nourishment and rest is essential. This is also a time when quiet academic pursuits need to be interspersed with whole-some physical activities. The principal who knows how to tell which pupils need which schedules at which times in their development will have a better school than the principal who ignores these pupil needs.

A tense inner-city school got a new principal, one who was committed to making desegregation work and to turning around the attitude of a hostile staff. He walked out to the front of his building as the buses and cars started arriving, shaking hands, introducing himself, and requiring that incoming students stop long enough to identify themselves. Over time, there were important con-versations about concerns and accomplishments which needed to be shared.

He greeted black and he greeted white. He greeted honor students and the barely educable. He greeted those who wanted to be greeted and those who did not. Soon the assistant principal joined him out front. It took a little pressure, but teachers began arriving early in their class-rooms in order to share with their pupils what was impor-tant to them.

The headmaster of an enormously prestigious indepen-dent boy's school regularly placed his chair smack dab in the middle of the central hall when the classes changed. He was daily given an updated book—a page for each boy. He perused this each morning before he moved to center hall, and as the boys flowed by, they were obliged to bid him a "Good morning," to meet his eye, and if singled out to stop for a word.

The boy who had learned of his grandfather's passing the day before got a kind and sympathetic word; the boy who had come in a disappointing second in the swim meet the previous weekend was encouraged to keep working on that backstroke; the boy who had been given a demerit for talking back to a houseparent was admonished to live up to his highest sense of chivalry.

The principal (headmaster) didn't teach, but he had an assistant principal who was a superb teacher and directed the academic rigor for the school. This hall sitter was a superb counselor, and watched over young boys as well as young faculty with an eagle eye. He also was a coach, and saw to it that coaching fairness came first.

I rather like this story about him, which I bothered to check for authenticity. It seems that no boy was allowed to graduate from this preparatory school without having swum the length of the pool. For one boy this had proven an elusive goal. His fear of the deep water cramped him into an inability to swim.

When the headmaster learned, toward the close of this boy's senior year, that he might not graduate because of this one snag, he came to the pool and asked the lad to come stand with him at the deep end.

He asked the boy if he was afraid. When the answer was yes, the headmaster responded, "Good." Then ordered: "Now, son, I'm going to push you into the deep end and you sink to the bottom and then run like hell, and don't start breathing until your head hits the air."

Accomplishment! We do not know if that boy ever got in the water again, but that's a mighty fine example of coaching by a principal. That's a good principal.

Principals as Diagnosticians

But let's come back to research. The alert principal wants to use diagnostic tests to find the weaknesses in his staff, and in what areas more time on task is needed. Here's one suggestion for improving principals' decisions about which basic skills need emphasizing.

Take all incoming students for junior and senior high schools, and in elementary schools, target grade four, and chart their test scores for each of the basic skills. Note the average for each group of students in spelling, vocabulary, arithmetic computation and problem-solving, study skills, and reading.

Which is the highest average for all these skills? Which is the lowest? What about the students who fall below the 20th percentile in the skill with the highest average; are they below the 20th percentile in all the others?

Let's assume that spelling and math problem-solving are the lowest averages for the fourth graders as well as for the students entering junior high; and that for the senior high tenth graders the low average is problem-solving and study skills. Let's also assume that the same fourth graders with the spelling problems are the ones with the math reasoning problems.

The "solution" is "easy." Just improve the teaching of spelling and math reasoning in the primary grades! Of course, that's an enormous task for any principal, but without the diagnostic testing and without some simple test analysis, no principal knows just where to place heavy emphasis, or which pupils might better be served by having more and possibly different teachers.

Let's assume that those incoming junior high pupils, with low averages for spelling and math reasoning are victims of too much "telling" on the part of teachers and too little "hands-on doing." A great many teachers learned to spell by memorizing, and they don't understand the needs of the pupil who needs to write and sound out each word several times before it's committed to memory.

Also, a lot of teachers fumbled their way through math problems in high school themselves, memorizing formulas and applying them almost at random until they worked. They have few teaching tricks in their repertoire to set up hands-on math challenges, and they try to force the children who could well solve a problem if they could work it out with graphs and counters and weights and balances, etc., to conceptualize mentally without using any materials.

Of course, the principal may find that time on task is the culprit. That the teachers in his system not only don't adjust teaching styles to learner needs, but that spelling lessons and practice get the shortest classroom time. Also, that math computation occurs regularly, but that math reasoning problems are presented only once a week.

The point is, obviously, that teaching would improve if the principal had some important data about what was and was not being learned to help him/her in making decisions about use of school time and resources.

It's not necessary for every principal to be a psychometrician. But every principal would be improved if he/she learned how to read test results, how to study those results in light of the school enrollment, and how to use limited financial resources wisely, making sure that sufficient funds go toward eliminating the academic low points.

I once was asked to analyze a 200-member teaching/coaching faculty for a small school district. I discovered that 101 of the 200 combined some athletic coaching with classroom teaching duties.

Some of the coaches were enormously disinterested academicians. I asked the high school principal if we could run a check on who was teaching those students who were falling regularly below grade level in math class.

I then asked if he had the records of those who had dropped out of school, and if he could find out who their math teachers had been. We then compared the records of the last two graduating classes (and dropouts from those classes) with who their math teachers had been.

We found, as you might expect, a self-fulfilling prophecy. The weakest math students coming into high school were put with the disciplinarian coaches who weren't skilled, caring teachers. The weak students, provided with competitive and punitive math classes—craving, instead, tender concern and strong coaching fell even further behind.

The math teacher coaches became progressively authoritarian, and the principal admitted that in no time in his ten-year career at the school had he ever expected one of these coaches to become better teachers. Yes, he admitted, they did get funds to go to coaching clinics; and no, he'd never thought to make them team teach with a skilled teacher of the learning disabled in order to learn how to get their pupils out of the academic cellar.

Was no tutoring provided at all for weaker students? My analysis went just one step deeper to find, of course, that tutoring was provided, but only for the varsity athletes who were having academic problems.

Was I encountering an exceptionally bad principal? Yes. But, is such a bleak picture true of some 10 percent of all 80,000 school principals? Of 20 percent?

What was interesting, for this high school principal, was that his desire for improvement did not come from uncovering this callousness about students with learning problems, but with costs. He was astounded when we turned his line budget into a program budget to discover what it cost to have a few tall boys play inter-school basketball in a rural area requiring miles of bus travel.

As we figured out what each varsity sport cost, and how much each academic class cost, it became obvious that some areas of the high school curriculum had been shamefully shortchanged.

To his enormous credit, he set about putting his academic house in order. Further, his school board began to understand the need to find how costs were related to teaching activities. And they began to hold the principal responsible not so much for staying within the line budget totals, but for distributing costs in relation to needs.

Parents are well within their rights to ask principals how costs are distributed among school activities. So are taxpayers. Many school systems have volunteer budget committees, and it's certainly within their charge to do the kind of fiscal analysis required by program budgeting.

Principals as Patrons of the Arts

Parents, too, have every right to question principals about their choices regarding activities for the students. Does your school have a debate team? And does the principal support the team by letting them compete locally, regionally, and nationally?

Does the school have an active theater program and do

the children regularly put on plays, have them critiqued, and compete locally, regionally, and perhaps statewide?

When was the last time the school put on an operetta? When was the last time the school attempted to include the least academically able pupils in an operetta?

Debaters learn how to read, how to write, how to reason, how to do library research, how to think on their feet, how to articulate thoughts, how to analyze, how to present ideas, how to organize material, and to broaden their vocabularies.

Would any principal wish to argue that these are not what his school is all about?

Many a school puts on one or two plays a year, but why so few? Aren't the very skills needed for a dramatization what schools are all about? And aren't some of the students who appear to give so much trouble in school the very ones who might come alive and alert if they were part of a production they believed in?

Certainly if children are to start school at age 4, and are to be completing their high school courses at age 14, debating and dramatics will be even more necessary, as these activities help younger pupils to get outside themselves. As the skills and qualities necessary for debate and drama prepare pupils for that important next step—either more schooling in college, or a work/study program at the secondary level.

When a controversial issue is tearing a school apart, those students in the vanguard might work out the script for a play in which they would perform. The principal might write himself/herself into the play. Let drama absorb some of the excess energy; let some of the heat surrounding the issue air out on a neutral platform.

If a public school building is ugly—and too many of them are—principals might locate all local professional sculptors, painters, carvers, weavers, potters, etc., and invite them to make available two or three items from which the students might choose one.

Probably the children shouldn't have to be restricted to those items which artists are willing to give away, but should be able to pay for what they would like to display at school. For this, the principal must lead the way to find the necessary funds.

What would these artistic purchases do besides enhance the beauty of the school? They will guide those principals, not already so inclined, to a deeper appreciation of local artistic talent. At the very least, they would alert the head of the school to focus attention on beauty, grace, symmetry, and loveliness.

Our children badly need their schools to lead them into an appreciation of all things beautiful. If we really do plan to make the school a launching pad for two years of national service, and if we plan to prepare students for either full-time college or part-time training combined with a part-time job, then we need the school setting to personify beauty and grace.

There's no reason why a principal couldn't appoint a group of students, yearly, to be on an arts acquisition committee, to provide funds for this committee, and to help them in choosing the artists whose works they will consider buying. There's every reason why children should learn to do this type of buying.

We've organized our school governments in very peculiar ways. Yes, many schools hold student elections and have some form of student government. And many classroom teachers organize so that there is a class president, vice-president, and maybe a secretary and treasurer. What's most curious about this "elective government" is that it appears from coast to coast and from border to border, yet there is no national prescription.

And even more curious yet is the fact that even in northern New England, where the town meeting is such a beloved, colorful moment for all the adults in a given town, almost no public school in those towns uses the town-meeting structure as its organizing governance.

Principals as Governors

The kind and type of government in place in each school building is, without question, the responsibility of the building principal.

Most schools are run autocratically; a few inner-city schools appear to take the form of military dictatorships, complete with armed guards patrolling halls.

The present structure, with class and school presidents apes club structure, not our national democracy. We need to devise ways for in-school government to parallel local, state, and national government in clear enough ways to help prepare our children for democracy as adults.

And we need to clarify for our children the concepts which underly democracy, and not just its form, such as is taught in civics classes.

Each principal is in charge of each school and hence directly in charge of seeing that concepts of democracy are not only taught, but, as far as possible, lived out in practice in the school. Schools could have a senate; each class acting as a state.

Rather than each class having a "president," each class group could elect two "senators." And these senators could join other class senators as part of the legislature, which in turn could establish some of the laws which govern that particular school.

Of course, there are laws which children have no business amending or dismissing; there's no question that authority lines in a public school must be governed by the adults. But there are many laws which could come before the school senate.

The U.S. Constitution provides not only for a senate, and the structuring of voting for that office, but also provides for what should happen if a senator does not uphold the laws he's sworn to uphold. School impeachment procedures might well follow those in our U.S. Constitution.

There would seem to be little reason in most school settings to have a two-house legislature, and it's conceivable that students would readily understand a structure which included only a senate, providing equal representation from essentially equally sized groups.

It would seem possible as well to create a justice department, and to use trial by a jury of peers.

Interestingly, many selective, independent boarding schools have in place such a judicial structure. When discipline cases come up before the principal (headmaster/ headmistress), selected students are permitted to be part of the review process. Often they influence the ultimate decision; often, too, they suggest the punishment to fit the crime.

Few public schools have such an organization in place, yet every single student needs to practice being part of a jury.

A school jury system could have a panel drawn by random selection. Both the prosecution and the defense could pick a jury from this panel and then "try" their case.

If each and every school principal did nothing more democratic than set up a senate and conduct trials by jury, holding an occasional town meeting to discuss and vote on all-school issues, they would revolutionize the way our children are prepared to participate in our government.

Of course, we should be doing a better job in the classroom teaching about the concepts of democracy, but each principal needs to put in place as much democratic practice as is feasible. Schools must be run by the adults who are ultimately responsible for the children therein, but, yes, principals are charged with training good citizens, and one way to provide that training is to provide a training ground.

It's no secret that among the established adult age groups in the United States, those in school and most recently out of school exercise their right to vote the least. Now, that lack of direct participation in democratic governance is often blamed on the "apathy" or "disinterest" of the young adult. Seldom do we hear that somehow it's the fault of the schools from which these young adults have emerged.

But isn't it our fault? Haven't our schools failed? It would be interesting to discover, when the results of the NAEP (National Assessment of Educational Progress) first came out and it was discovered how little young adults remembered about the structure of our democratic form of government and how few had even voted, what steps each high school principal took to find out how his recent graduates and school-leavers had done.

It would be interesting to discover what changes principals made in not only what was taught but how democratic principles were played out within their buildings in order to stimulate their high schoolers to want to vote; to want to be part of our political process.

There's a further very curious "right" which many educators have been given or given to themselves. And this is the "right" not to serve on jury duty. In many states, teachers are exempt from jury duty.

Good heavens! Here we have those whose charge it is to prepare our children for full citizenship in both participatory and representative government never having experienced what it is to serve with a jury of peers judging the behavior of a peer.

Principals should see to it that their teachers are freed to serve on jury duty; should plan their staffing so that a few of the teachers may be gone for specific periods each year. Principals, too, should plan time so that they can serve on jury duty once in at least every five years.

The principal who plans to let pupils choose an original piece of art to place in the building could let the final selection come out of a town meeting. Like jury duty, voting at town meeting is direct participatory democracy. There are so few decisions children may make, and so many that adults must make for them, that it takes considerable energy and imagination on the part of each school principal to find ways to engage pupils in democratic behavior.

Principals as Carers

Suppose we really do start our children in school at the age of 4, and expect that they will complete the basic course by the age of 14. How much more important it will be to get across both the forms and concepts of democratic living.

Then those students aged 14–15 who stay on for cooperative education (alternating skill training in school with on-the-job training in a business) could and should take many of the leadership positions in the school senate and a department of justice.

And those between the ages of 16 and 26 who have

chosen a school setting for doing their national service would be practicing (beginning at age 18) democracy as an adult and supervising efforts at democratic living carried out by children and growing adults.

And further, since it's the schools which will be keeping track of their graduates and supervising (approving and helping locate) their two years of national service, principals will be in a much better place to know just how well their school programs have, in fact, prepared their students for participatory citizenship.

Today, we have almost no mechanisms for tracking what happens to students who leave our secondary schools. Most school counselors never follow the immediate careers of those who leave school and do not go directly into a college or university. And any further information generally is available only if the former student takes the initiative to let the secondary school know where he/she is and what he/she is doing.

And even if school-leavers provide this information, it has no place to go within the present school structure. But, should secondary schools be in charge of national service, and should the age of 26 be the last for that service, we would be able to put in place longitudinal studies providing us with the very information we have always needed.

Are our schools doing the job needed? What needs changing? What needs improving? What needs eliminating? What needs adding? All good questions; all need answers.

The school which sees itself as college preparatory generally knows today what percentage of its graduates are accepted by an institution of higher learning. But it seldom keeps track of them in any formal way past that first acceptance.

The principal of such a school, at the very least, could put in place a way to find out how well each graduate feels he was prepared for college; what value he now places on the information he got from his counselor; and what his success has been based on what he prepared for it to be.

If colleges and universities require a certain level of competence in a foreign language for entrance, then today's secondary school principals offer language training.

Would that principals considered preparing students for good citizenship at the same level of responsibility; would that principals thought job preparation was so important that no student should take on a full-time job until he/she had carried out part-time job responsibilities under the guidance of the school and with supportive academic training geared directly to the job's requirements.

Would that principals of primary and elementary schools accepted responsibility for whether the children who attend their institutions learn to read, write, compute, and quantify.

By this I mean, really accept that responsibility. Test to find out if all children are learning these skills. Test to find out if teachers are reaching out with the same skill and enthusiasm to teach every pupil regardless of race, religion, color, social standing in the community, and quickness in the classroom.

All elementary school principals should test whether both the atmosphere and the amount of skill learning don't improve by accepting local children into the first grade when home and school feel they are ready for this step, regardless of the calendar date or the age of the child.

Principals should test whether family groupings (mixed-age groups) in these beginners' classrooms don't provide not only a better ethos, but more actual learning. If little ones can help even littler ones, and if all the children in a classroom are expected to help out all the other kids as well as the teacher, won't it follow that they all will learn more?

The teacher with a family grouping will want some aides (volunteer or paid), and most teachers, once they experience the success of this multi-age atmosphere, want to include student teachers, senior citizens, talented townspeople, and older school pupils in their program flow.

It is well nigh impossible for teachers to try out all these radical (or so they seem at first) ideas without the full cooperation of a principal who not only is sympathetic, but a participant. The classroom which is family grouped needs different supplies, multi-size desks, works on its own time schedule, uses more out-of-classroom space, wants to issue special reports to parents.

If little four-year-olds are really going to come to school when they are ready and not when it's September, then the principal is going to have to have some system for determining which four-year-olds should enter when their parents think they are ready and which should wait until the school thinks they are ready.

Principals as Directors

The principal who wants a classroom to be designed into learning centers and chock full of games and learning materials, who thinks its important for every classroom to have a stage area for the putting on of skits and plays, who believes little children should spend as much time out of doors as possible tending gardens, doing outdoor building projects, using playground and park areas for nature study and beginning basic research skills—this principal is going to have to lead the teaching staff every step of the way.

This principal is going to have to be the one to explain to parents how this radical tangent from the traditional is supposed to work and why the school staff feels it's better than the lockstep past.

This principal is going to have to be the one to help the reluctant older teacher or the newly trained college graduate see how they can adapt to such a change.

Today, a great many teachers who want to try new ideas just close the classroom doors and plunge ahead on their own. But there is only so much change possible without involving the top administration both of a building and of a school system.

In fact, the main reason so many very exciting reforms have failed to make significant changes in schools and schooling is that so few principals have led the way. Instead, much of the banner-carrying has been done by parents (who, when thoroughly discouraged, opt out of the public sector for the private), or by teachers (who, when not backed up in their efforts at improvement, complain of burnout, and either switch to a nonpublic school or to some other profession).

In all fairness, principals have a great many more constituencies than teachers. Principals must answer to layers of administrators—the number of layers appears to be in direct proportion to the size of the budget—as well as to a school board. They must attend to each and every parent, and, unless they have delegated the authority, must run a restaurant, supply room, bus system, recreation department, etc., etc.

And to further complicate the life of a principal, the buildings they have been asked to administer have been built too large and house too many children—so many children that the principal is not able to know each child personally. A great many principals, faced with this dilemma, have broken the student body into smaller sections, putting a "houseparent" or vice-principal or dean or . . . in charge of each section.

Our school-age population is a small one today, but not tomorrow. We've only got a few short years in which to correct the institutional nature of our school buildings. Somehow, a whole nation needs to be convinced that a 500-pupil high school and a 300-pupil elementary school are the best or optimum sizes.

Somehow a whole nation needs to be convinced that schools of that size are not fiscally extravagant, but economically sound. And further, that each school building should house other community services. Again, if a town is going to place branch libraries (and support personnel) in public school buildings, it's the principals in that town who will have to lead the way.

If school buildings are going to house public health and welfare officials, staff from the Army Corps of Engineers in charge of the local dam site and related recreation area, a local or state police substation, and provide lunches for senior citizens—it's the principals in each town who must coordinate this blend of services.

It's possible, of course, for the school board to decide they want school buildings to house smaller enrollments, and for compatible services to be housed in sections of each school. They can order the superintendent to make this happen. And the superintendent and his staff can enlist the principals in carrying out this order. Which gets us right back to building principals. And how much more smoothly such changes would come about were the principals to be in on the reform from the start.

A good many parents, subscribing to the notion of survival of the fittest, are pleased when they discover their local public school is run along competitive lines. Yet cooperation not only lets the fittest survive, but it raises the whole population, and makes the United States a better place for us all. If there are winners, there must be losers. And at the present time, a great many schools have fewer winners than losers.

And that's expensive; enormously expensive. The winners generally become productive members of society; their contributions are positive and enhance our democratic way of life. The losers, handicapped as they start adulthood, falter and flounder—the worst requiring institutionalizing in a penal colony. From them is taken the right to vote as well as the right to earn an independent living.

Our competitive schools have managed to support our welfare system so that those brought up in a welfare-supported home see no way out of establishing such a home for themselves. Few children brought up in welfare homes break out of that cycle of poverty. Their one chance is their local public schools. The one person in town charged with the responsibility to find a way to intersect generational welfare dependency is the school principal.

That's not the job of welfare departments—they are to provide the necessary services. It's the principal who must create an atmosphere of learning and a desire for improvement (as well as all necessary skill training) which counters the downward trend of the home. There are those who think the "solution" is to take away the food stamps and welfare payments.

But this is cruel in the extreme. Children have no way to support themselves, and more than three-fourths of all welfare payments are directed to the school-age population. No, it's schooling which is the first and last solution to welfare dependency. Schooling which is supportive; schooling which is compensatory; schooling which is so persuasive that it cuts through the clouds of discouragement and ignorance in many a welfare home.

School principals know this; so do kindergarten teachers.

Principals as Desegregators

The superintendent of a middle-size school district (about 10 percent of the homes on welfare) was talking with a kindergarten teacher one day, lamenting the fact that a boy whom he thought had great promise had just dropped out of school three months before graduation. The teacher told him she wasn't surprised. "How come?" he asked.

She explained that he'd started school with a chip on his shoulder and that every classmate with parents who could help with homework and mete out needed discipline had beaten him in the "race." Therefore, rather than "lose" the race, he'd saved face and dropped out.

"Got any more like that in your kindergarten?" Of course she answered in the affirmative. "What can you do about it?" She gave him an earful!

To summarize: it was all the superintendent's fault. He and the principals were all full of rank-in-class and high achievers. All full of statistics about which pupils got into which selective colleges. All full of who knew who at the country club. All full of winning athletic teams, award-winning marching bands, and prestigious debate squads.

"How," she asked, "are these little ones to ever succeed if success comes from getting on the fast track early?"

If each pupil in a school is going to be respected as an individual, this respect must start with the principal. And for each pupil, the treatment must be just a little different. The master teacher knows this, and often what little gain a child makes comes from the efforts of a caring teacher. But if the whole school is run by a principal who disregards helping the tender and needy, the efforts of a single teacher often dissipate in the hallways.

It was a very old school building in an old whites-only neighborhood. To desegregate the school district, this school was lumped with several others covering a wide enough attendance area to include a mix of races, religions, colors, interests, and so forth.

The newly assigned principal, after watching the problems from a spot in the central administration the first year of the mixed enrollment changes, determined to reach out into the community for support.

She walked the area after school, picking a block, and stopping to talk with whomever she could find at home.

Almost to an older adult, they had never met whoever had been principal of the school; certainly none had ever had the principal pay a "courtesy call." And they were not only interested in hearing about the school's program, but at the close of each visit the principal heard neighbors saying, "If I can do anything, let me know."

She wasn't much different from most principals she knew, and the first 30 or 40 visits she sort of chuckled at the neighborhood residents' naiveté—after all, she was the professional educator, and she knew precisely how she was going to run her school.

When she decided that the old fixed-equipment playground needed modernizing, she realized the neighbors were going to be inconvenienced with heavy grading equipment, noise, and dirt.

Principals as Catalysts

The fifth and sixth graders were formed into informations quads, and each prepared a community brochure to let their portion of the neighborhood know what was planned for the playground. They took the flyers and brochures from house to house. And they kept coming back to school saying such things as "the lady in the big brown house says she'll come to school if we want her to." Also, "You know the man with the double garage? He has lots of tools in there and he says he'll teach woodworking here if we want to learn how. Can he come?"

As the principal explained, "I didn't need a brick wall to fall on me, but nearly! I went to talk to the man with the woodworking tools in his garage, and told him how sad I was that our school didn't have a woodworking room." It seems that he had gone to the school as a boy, knew there was an ideal spot for a workshop in the basement, and to cut this story short, headed up a very active woodworking program in conjunction with about 20 other neighborhood carpenters.

Before that first school year was out, the children had "adopted" a nearby nursing home, going there to entertain with songs and skits; to deliver valentines; to help those in the home write letters; to decorate their rooms with drawings and posters; to tell them what was happening at school; to read to them; to make them bed socks.

And several days a week older neighborhood residents came in to visit with their special pupil, one-on-one. Parchesi, Monopoly, Scrabble, endless card games, jig-saw puzzles, jacks, hand crafts, even harmonica-playing were the order of the day through the lunch period. The older folks came to do their "things," and the pupils matched themselves up.

A sewing room became a necessity, and little ones with limited home budgets learned how to stretch a wardrobe. They not only learned how to mend, but a big box of hand-me-downs appeared and whole new outfits could be "borrowed."

For many of the older people, it was their first opportunity to get to know children from different ethnic backgrounds. And they freely admitted to loving the school, saw it as a part of their neighborhood, and wanted to feel it was still "theirs."

Many children today come from single parent families. Often there is a need for a boy or girl to get to know a man (or woman) in a kind of big brother or big sister relationship. Many mature men and women would willingly be a mentor to a boy or girl in need. The alert principal could be the catalyst for this matchmaking.

A program in a large Eastern city provides a business man or woman for every 15-year-old potential dropout. These mentors are not allowed to share money; their expertise is called on. The hope is that the pupils will become interested in going on to college, which means finishing high school.

Where the school principals have actively pursued this program, it has flourished; where they have only tolerated it, it has floundered.

Too many schools use bell systems and loudspeakers for all-school announcements. This intrusion is symptomatic of a lack of caring, a lack of democracy, a lack of feeling. Classes can start and finish without bells; notices can be shared without imposing them wholesale throughout a loudspeaker system.

I willingly tell this story on myself. I discovered one day that the principal of an elementary school in which I was teaching grade five, regularly listened in on my classroom through the loudspeaker system. One of my pupils told me he could hear the "click" when the principal tuned in.

I made a deal with him; the moment he heard the telltale click, he was to stand up and point to the loudspeaker, but not to speak. As soon as I saw him do this, I was to clear my throat. When the children saw him standing and pointing and heard me clear my throat, no matter what any of them was doing, they were to sit down and open a library book and begin reading silently.

We would remain that way until our pointer signalled that the loudspeaker had "clicked" off by sitting down. We would then resume whatever we had been doing. That happened for several days in a row. Finally the principal took to tuning in, then tuning out, then walking up two flights of stairs and down the hall to pass our room.

By the time he'd done that, we'd be back to our noisy selves, with pupils scattered all around the room in learning stations. I was unable to convince him that he should stop intruding on our class, either by silent listening or by giving announcements. Nor was he able to convince me that letting the pupils learn at their own pace and through the use of many hands-on activities was bad for them.

In another school system, some several years later, I had a delightful building principal. He had agreed to team teach with me in order to learn some new math. Again, I had a pupil with a sharp ear. This lad could tell me when Dr. R——— was striding down the hall, and we'd sometimes plan surprises for him with some math puzzle.

My pupil was able to teach me to recognize the same sharp, definite tread, so much so that years later in a different town on the fourth floor of the east wing of a private hospital, while visiting a patient, I heard that tread, stepped to the doorway, and my "old" principal and I had a good visit.

What a difference between those two men! One was looking for trouble; the other looking for ways to learn and to help others to learn. One building had a tense and forbidding atmosphere; the other was comfortable and at moments academically exciting.

The principal sets the tone for courtesy in a building. The more courteous the better for all concerned. It's the principal who either establishes line authority, or works out of a circle of understanding.

It's the principal who should be hiring new teachers as interns; should be setting up seminars and workshops for them; should be helping them out by team teaching with them; should be evaluating them. It's the principal who should be deciding which of the interns might be invited to stay in the school system—if not that principal's school.

It's the principal who should help evaluate teachers on the basis of the quality of their teaching.

Every time merit pay is suggested, the argument goes that there's no one who can tell a good teacher from a bad one; no one free enough of prejudice and nepotism to make a sound judgment about who should be paid more for a superior teaching job. Of course there's someone who could do all that—the principal.

And the principal who argues that he or she is not qualified to evaluate teachers and teaching should probably be asked to stop being a principal. Every principal can set up criteria in conjunction with the teaching staff, and determine how those criteria are to be judged. And then each principal can be part of the team that makes the judgments about which interns to keep, which teachers to remove from classroom duties, which ones to pay token salaries, and which ones to designate as master teachers and to pay accordingly.

It's certainly possible that if a principal was to do an excellent job of attracting and keeping only excellent teachers his/her school would cost more per pupil than some other school. Would this be so bad? Isn't what is going on now—no evaluation and poor teachers in control in many classes—worse?

And now one final suggestion for principals— particularly those who feel they're running a good school. Ask the parents to do an evaluation on their own. Ask them not only to evaluate the principal as manager/as teacher/as counselor/as fiscal officer/as restauranteur/as playground supervisor/as gardener/as bus scheduler, but to evaluate the ethos of the school. Is this principal's school a pleasant place to study and learn?

Checklist

1.   *Learning:* Broaden your academic base; read and discuss serious literature; learn a language; become an historian.

2.   *Coaching:* Read aloud to selected students; coach your teachers; reassign staff in relation to their effectiveness.

3.   *Budgeting:* Turn your line item budget into program categories; delegate all housekeeping (i.e., nonacademic duties).

4.   *Researching:* Find out how effective your school is and adjust curriculum, teaching assignments, pay differentials, peer teaching, athletics, counseling, etc., in light of what you have learned.

5. *Disciplining:* Improve your teachers: pair the weak with the strong; make them study physics; evaluate them as professionals; remove the unteachable from classrooms.

6. *Beautifying:* Invite artists to donate works; form student-run art acquisition teams; support active dance, music, theater programs.

7. *Governing:* Hold town meetings; set up a representative student senate; hold trials by jury to settle selected discipline cases; release teachers for community jury duty.

8. *Counseling:* Help set up the national service counseling program; do follow-up studies on graduates; get to know a few students each day.

9. *Sharing:* Provide special help to children living in welfare-supported homes; walk your neighborhood; share school facilities with the town library, public health and police officials; welcome volunteers of every age to share skills and interest with all pupils.

Parents: You can check out your school principal with this list. Is he/she a good learner, coach, budgeter, researcher, disciplinarian, beautifier, governor, counselor, and sharer? And your child's principal can check you out as well: just how willing have you been to help with that learning, coaching, beautifying, counseling, and sharing?

School board members, trustees, and superintendents: This checklist, while apparently aimed at the building principal, is really targeted on you. Just what do you want your building principals to be? Are they glorified housekeepers, or are they the academic leaders in each community? They need your guidance, direction, and support.

Teachers: You, too, will need to support any principal who wants to improve, particularly one who recognizes his/her role as a master teacher and must choose someone else to take care of administrative details.

Principals: Does your building "hum?" Is your teachers' room full of lively debate? Do you regularly hold discussions with some of the scholars in town? Are you substituting at least once a week for an hour in a classroom?

Do you meet your students on the front steps or in the hallways, greeting them not only by name, but showing that you know what's on their minds? But most of all, do you know the ethos or feeling in your school, and if it isn't joyous and healthy are you doing something about it?

Introduction to Chapter Four

Improving Discipline

By Schuyler M. Meyer, Jr.

President, Edwin Gould Foundation for Children
New York City, New York

A year or so ago a major United States city was seeking a top educator to head its school system. At a large public meeting the three leading candidates were asked what they would do about the serious problem of discipline. Two talked of more police, more armed guards, computerizing offenses, more expelling of bad students. The third and successful candidate talked of measures he would undertake to improve the school's "ethos," to use Cynthia Parsons' word. He never mentioned police.

A small group with which I am associated is talking of designing an "ideal" school. We struggled a whole afternoon to define the objectives, goals, philosophy of an "ideal" school. Suddenly the answer came. It was to be a school the students *wanted* to attend. There's the "ethos" again!

The discipline problems are most critical in schools in largely minority and poor areas. School has little meaning for many of these young people. It is immoral that we permit the climate of so many public schools to force minority young to drop out of school, virtually illiterate, with little hope of a productive, happy life. The tragic unemployment rate of uneducated minority youth in our cities is well known. How many people realize that the unemployment rate of American Indian youth on some reservations reaches 80 to 90 percent? What a terrible waste of a valuable resource!

Cynthia Parsons' solution to the discipline problem—"To have an imaginative and exciting school requir[ing] the hum of creativity; the buzz of busyness; the shouting for joy; dancing in the halls; singing in the locker room showers." What a joyous description!

Chapter Four
Improving Discipline

If there's one impression about U.S. public schools held by nearly every citizen, it's that there's not enough discipline. Year after year, those polled by Gallup, as well as by others, cite "discipline" as the No. 1 school problem—discipline, mind you, takes precedence over drugs, drinking, curriculum content, preparation of teachers, salary structures, exploitation of athletes, unionism, and so on.

When nonpublic schools are compared with public institutions, discipline ranks high on the list of reasons why a family chooses to send a child "away" to school, or to pay tuition when the local public school is free.

A great many of the discipline problems in public schools are not due to inherently incorrigible children, but often can be traced to the way children are treated by the school and by fellow pupils.

Curiously, hundreds (perhaps thousands) of our schools are run more in the mode of military dictatorships than of friendly, democratic communities. Competition in the classroom, in the gymnasium, and in the social milieu dictates that there will be an "in" as well as an "out" group. Merits and demerits abound in such environments, and the weak pupil becomes either withdrawn or belligerent as a reaction to the oppressive atmosphere.

Ethnic minorities, particularly, have to fight against many odds to get a fair chance at the starting line.

Management by intimidation, when it attempts to crush all in its path from the superintendent's office to the principal's building to the teacher's classroom, produces more unruly behavior than it ever stops.

116

Hard to get that across to bullies. Hard to get that across to those who hear what they want to hear and see what they want to see.

Hard to get that across to the teacher who likes to boast about the number of students he or she flunks; and equally hard to get across to the principal who boasts about the number of pupils on suspension.

Discipline & Self-Esteem

A good many pupils start to fail in school before grade five. They are identifiable because their academic needs are so great. And unless extraordinary measures are taken to remediate, the school then has a problem on its hands.

The problem: How to keep from being a discipline problem the pupil whose school day is made up of failure after failure. That's a lot to ask of a smart, growing young person.

Let's suppose the lessons to be taught were connected with swimming and not the 3 Rs. And let's assume that an enthusiastic little five-year-old were to arrive at the pool in early September, spend a whole year taking swimming lessons, and at the end of that year not have graduated from the shallow end of the pool.

Let's assume that the same youngster tries for two more years to learn how to swim, and doesn't get past the back float stage. Now it's the fourth year, and a nine-year-old is told to go to the pool with dozens of other nine-year-olds, most of whom enjoy swimming and are allowed in the deep end.

We can assume that the non-swimmer will try to get out of going to the pool; and if that doesn't work, try to stall getting from the locker room to poolside.

Now, let's further assume that the swimming school is competitive. Teachers are primarily interested in working with those who learn to swim quickly and well; and punish those who aren't as quick as the others. Also let's assume that the teachers welcome teasing and peer pressure from good swimmers as a goad to the poor swimmers.

You can readily see that you'd have a discipline problem; you'd not only have several withdrawn children, but a good many who would "act out" their frustration. You'd have to work out ways to keep the non-swimmers busy. You would not, of course, put the best swimming coaches with these pupils, but would relegate the neophytes and the poor coaches to these dregs.

And you would put in place punishments and rewards to make the pool a pleasant place for the best of the best to do their best. If you could afford it, you'd even have a second pool just for these non-swimmers—a pool, perhaps, which didn't even have a deep end (no college-prep classes for this bunch of dummies).

You wouldn't conduct school business within the town meeting format, but by directives from principals, vice-principals, department heads, and athletic directors. You certainly wouldn't build up an awards structure to honor non-swimmers; but would so arrange awards classifications that a mere handful of the best swimmers would qualify.

Perhaps I've already overworked the analogy. But what's important to realize is that most school discipline problems stem from the way school is kept and not because every fifth kid is some kind of "rotter."

The list of reasons why children are discipline problems has grown by leaps and bounds in the past decade.

The National Education Association (covering for more than a million teachers) is fond of quoting statistics about how many parents are alcoholics, how many are single parents, how many are culturally deprived, how many are child abusers, how many are not fluent in English—all to argue that the job is well nigh "impossible."

Discipline & Magic

A friend of mine took on the job of being education editor for a daily newspaper in a very large school district. He asked me how he could tell a "good" from a "bad" teacher. And how he could get a handle on school discipline problems.

I told him to take the first month on the job and to spend one hour each morning visiting two classrooms in a different school each day. To pick the rooms at random, and to vary the visits to elementary, middle, junior and senior high schools.

He did as I suggested. He stayed a half hour in each classroom he visited, and in 20 school days spent some time in as many schools and made sure he sat in on every grade level. We talked at the end of this time.

Yes, he said, by the second week he could tell what the principal was going to be like before he actually got in the building. And could tell if that principal was or was not in control of the pupils.

But what astounded him was the fact that he couldn't tell by sight, or even in the first five minutes in a classroom, whether he was going to watch a wicked (his word) teacher, an ordinary one (the vast majority), or be in a room full of magic (his word).

Magic was how he categorized the teachers who were in complete control, who showered love on the pupils, who couldn't think of enough reasons to shower it right back; teachers who saw to it that every child learned what the fastest seemed to absorb by osmosis.

No, all magic teachers weren't strict and sharp; all magic teachers weren't soft and cuddly; all magic teachers weren't clever academicians; all magic teachers weren't full of obvious teaching tricks.

He confessed he was often fooled by the look and style of a teacher during the opening moments of a class, but when that magic started to happen he said he could not only feel it, but touch it. He said in the presence of teaching magic, he would smile, and more often than not was late to the next class because he forgot to watch the clock.

There weren't any discipline problems in the magic classrooms, yet he observed that some of the same pupils, with wicked or ordinary teachers, engaged in deviant behavior (chaos was his word). The simple conclusion one is eager to draw after making such an observation is that schools with excellent teachers have no discipline problems.

But even the best teachers will admit that some students some of the time just are too ornery for ordinary controls. Of course, some of that orneriness comes from being shuttled between affection and cynicism, classroom to classroom.

My first year as a senior counselor in a well-run summer camp, the director stated during orientation: "If you find that the first three people you meet one morning are all crabby and out of sorts, you need some sleep." How others behave in our presence is, of course, the result of our own thinking—not of theirs.

That's what the "magic" teachers told my friend; they explained how they were responsible for the ethos in their classrooms; were responsible for how the kids thought about themselves.

Discipline & Imagination

In another city, in an experimental school for sixth graders, there were six teachers and some 225 pupils. Each student spent some time each day with each of the six teachers. Three of the teachers were imaginative and exciting people, loved to teach, and treated the pupil who didn't learn on the first try as a delightful challenge. Three of the teachers (first year for one of them) weren't terribly interested in the subjects they were teaching, gave a great deal of seat work, openly favored certain few children in each class group, and used grades as punishments and rewards.

It was incredible to watch nearly 200 Jekylls and Hydes struggle through each school day. The very same pupils would go from room to room, teacher to teacher, angelic in one setting; devilish in another. That is, all but one boy who defied all six teachers plus the principal.

That one lad required extraordinary measures. Finally came a series of suspensions lasting for a day or two, and isolation within the school setting. When they only stifled but did not cure him, it was decided to pair him up with a calming influence. A boy not nearly as academically quick. This was thought of as a "last resort," and should have been a first resort. It worked. Saddled with having to take the same grade in each subject as his buddy, he settled down, and while he did not stop being a bully was at least a pleasant bully.

In yet another school, this time with a 16-year-old, the problem was a lad who had not really learned to read and write, and was now confined to talking answers to homework questions into a tape recorder and then hoping his teachers would take the extra time to listen and give him passing grades.

Being functionally illiterate in a school devoted to getting everyone into college had thrown him into open rebellion with himself and everyone he contacted. He did not shave, bathe, or speak in anything but four-letter words. His clothes were rags; his attitude abrasive, and he was the only one who could fix a piece of playground equipment which ran on a gasoline engine and baling wire.

He had been tutored in the basic study skills along the way several times, and each teacher had come away from the sessions stating they had never known a ruder boy or one less likely ever to learn to read and write. Finally, as his high school teachers told him they would listen no longer to his tape recordings and that he would be failed if he did not turn in legible and mature papers, he pled for a tutor.

A graduate student said she'd take on the task. She correctly surmised that he learned kinesthetically, and that he needed to do some tracing of simple words; further, that he needed to believe he really could ever learn to read and write at the level of his sophisticated thinking.

She planned the very first tutoring session so that at the end of less than four minutes she stated: "Thanks, Dave, that's all."

For perhaps the first time in his life, the teacher was quitting before he got a chance to do so. He was tracing his name at the time. She took the paper, crumpled it, and threw it into the wastebasket. All the while she was saying, "That was a very good session. Thank you for your cooperation. See you tomorrow at the same time."

He couldn't believe what was happening to him. He tried to stay, but she left the room. He hadn't learned even how to write his name, yet the four minutes had been pleasant.

The next morning the teacher again cut the lesson off after less than 15 minutes, but not before several words were traced and he had begun to move his finger in the air without having it shake.

The third morning he was clean-shaven, and was wearing a new shirt. But his language was still foul; his teeth unbrushed; his breath unpleasant. His tutor appeared not to notice, instead continued the tracing efforts first with crayon on strips of stiff paper, then in the air, then on the desk top, and finally writing with chalk on the board.

She waited until the close of the lesson, this time a regular length, and then commented on his partial cleanliness, ignoring the rough spots. But she asked about the language; said it offended her. But offered, if he particularly wished to, to teach him how to spell some of the worst of his language habits.

Any teacher who ever had worked with him would have been astounded at what happened next:

The tears spilled out in a rush as he explained how difficult it had been to sit on the sidelines while others he considered no brighter had understood so easily what had remained a mystery to him. The teacher waited until he got himself under control, and then issued a promise: "It's my job to teach you, and I will. I guarantee you will learn; I'm already pleased with our progress."

Now, he began to improve within days and in the next few weeks was attempting to write papers in class. Incredibly, teachers who had been giving him courtesy passing grades prior to this forward leap now began giving him failing grades and making fun of him in class as he performed far below grade level.

The controlled behavior began to break down, until the tutor got the principal to intervene and beg the teachers to give him time to catch up with himself.

His fellow students didn't need any such reprimanding. They began immediately to react positively to his new view of himself and of his abilities. They began to include him in discussion groups, and in the spring of that year voted him student body president for the following year.

From the worst discipline case on campus to an exemplary student leader—all because he was finally learning to read and write.

Dave's needs were extreme, but the solution to that discipline problem was not more punishment but better teaching. When probation officers who deal with juvenile offenders are asked about their charges, they are ready to point a finger in the direction of the school; to an atmosphere which nurtured hate and distrust and frustration and anger.

Discipline & Rewards

The rewards which are generally given only to the "top" students are the very rewards needed to lift the worst out of their storm centers. The rebellious student needs to be in the school play; needs to play a part which allows him to vent some of that emotion in a setting in which he can learn to see himself in perspective.

The rebellious academician needs to excel in a sport—if it's nothing more exciting than pool or bowling—and to feel that thrill which comes from trying and winning.

The troubled student needs to be given the opportunity to work with little pupils who are frustrated and having learning difficulty.

A delightful teacher, forced into retirement in one school community was able to add five more years to her teaching career by moving to another district. She taught chemistry, and the very first day in her new high school she was faced with the school troublemaker.

The faculty were amazed at her solution to the problem. He was made her assistant. Was put in charge of all equipment, and assigned to teach the chemistry section of general science to a junior high class. He stayed after school to help her prepare for the next day's lessons. He stayed after to help her take homework papers to her car.

He taught the junior high pupils with an iron rod and a

love of chemistry which had them begging for more time in the chem lab.

Going back a moment to the education editor who made 40 classroom visits while he was fresh on the job, he said there were times, even at the end of his month of school visits, when he couldn't tell at first whether the "chaos" he was observing in the classroom was from "magic" or from basic lack of control. He said it took less than ten minutes to know the difference, but in discussion with the principals of the schools he discovered that many of them didn't really know the difference and were trying to apply "standards" to keep all chaos to a minimum—never mind that in a few classrooms it was the heart and soul of excellent teaching.

A good teacher runs a multi-pupil circus, and generally has a good many aides working the classroom with her/him. A good teacher allows a flow of pupils in and out of the classroom, and encourages pupils helping pupils.

A poor teacher, fearing the loss of control, doesn't know how to deploy aides; tries to force pupils not to talk with each other much less deliberately work together.

If all the pupils in a given class are seated and quiet, that's not, necessarily, a disciplined class. It may be a stifled class; it may be a bored class. It can, of course, be a class which is undertaking some activity which is best done silently and seated! But not all that appears as chaos should be termed chaos.

To have an imaginative and exciting school requires the hum of creativity; the buzz of busyness; the shouting for joy; dancing in the halls; singing in the locker room showers.

Discipline & Sensitivity

A young friend of mine—born into fourth-generation welfare—went off to school at the age of six to start first grade. He stopped in to see me at the end of the week.

"Well, how did it go?"

"Twarn't no good."

"How come?"

"She never asked me nothing I know and kept telling me to sit down and to sit up."

"What were you doing when she told you to sit down?"

"I was looking out the window at a bulldozer."

"What were you doing when she told you to sit up?"

"I was lying on the floor 'cause I was tired."

"What did you want to tell her that you knew?"

"I could have told her about our bull, and how to tell poison ivy, and how to tell a Chevvy from a Ford."

Actually, he was lying on the floor because he was both tired and hungry. No meals were fixed in his home; no one was up and fixing him a good breakfast and mentally preparing him for a day at school in the early morning. No one in his family expected him to get along in school or to like it any better than they had. They weren't making any effort to compensate him for their lack of scholarship.

For him to have succeeded in school, the school would have had (he didn't make it past grade eight) to do the compensating. A sensitive teacher would have understood how much it would mean to such a lad to be able to watch a bulldozer at work. Furthermore, would have found he could have learned many reading and writing lessons had the bulldozer been the focus of his literary efforts.

A sensitive school would have seen to it that the breakfast he missed was supplied at school; a sensitive staff would have understood that he needed the mental pre-preparation as badly as the calories to be able to go through a day of academic concentration. And a well-run school would have varied his program, giving him plenty of physical exercise (through dance and music and games) without placing him in a competitive setting.

When the teacher was asked why she didn't let him tell about his bull, use his knowledge of plants and cars to stimulate an interest in reading, and recognize his hunger pangs, she had a ready answer.

"I know his family. Good for nothings, all of them."

He wasn't black and she white; the teacher wasn't an Anglo and the pupil Hispanic. She wasn't a member of one church and his family another. For her, resentful at earning a salary not far above the "free ride" poverty level, he was poor and that was enough.

In a few short years, the script which started in the first week of grade one was played out: Homework undone; inattentive in class; caught smoking; suspicion of pot; late to class; talking; disturbing; lost books; sometimes silence, other times open defiance.

Finally: Dropout.

He was in a small school district with only one elementary and one secondary school. A few of the larger school districts have found a partial answer to discipline problems; to the problem of how to reach hard-to-teach learners. They operate an "alternative" school.

Discipline & Alternatives

Interestingly, many of the methods for organizing these buildings point the way most, if not all, schools should be operated. Generally, an effort is made to engage troubled teenagers in the governance of the school, to put them under contract so that they actively agree to what it is they want to learn, at what pace, and toward what end.

The school with a senate—two representatives from each class group—and with a jury of peers to decide discipline cases, and with a town meeting format for all-school decisions is the school whose sense of democracy goes a long way toward meeting students where they need to be met. At fairness. At equity. At self-government.

Some "alternative" schools are for "deviants," for those whose behavior requires that they no longer attend the "regular" school. Some are for those with a special interest, such as a school focusing on creative arts, or math/science, or pre-college, pre-professional training.

There's no reason, of course, why one school could not house such alternatives under one roof. There really is no reason why schools do not offer real alternatives right from the start.

If one set of pupils would thrive in a family-grouped primary-grade class; and another group would enjoy the self-contained graded class; and another would like an almost individualized approach using computers, educational television, filmstrips, controlled readers, and other educational hardware, then why not offer as many alternatives as possible given the ability of the faculty and interests of the students and their parents.

If school were to start at the age of 4 and all pupils were to complete secondary school at the age of 14 or 15, there would be fewer opportunities for these youngsters to become discipline problems—at least in junior or senior high school. That is, if the school presents alternatives, the teaching is both exciting and demanding, a good mix of physical and mental activities takes place hourly, and pupils know what the goal is at the end of the basic school years.

This would shift older teenagers into one of two programs: either they would be in college or they would be in a cooperative education program alternating periods of study with on-the-job training. This would require colleges to provide a whole host of support services.

Many parents, of course, would keep more of these youngsters at home, sending them to a nearby college or university. But, selective colleges, wanting bright academically oriented youngsters would, as college-preparatory schools now do, provide supervised dormitory living arrangments to protect these pre-adults.

For those youngsters who do not go on to college, and who, instead, stay in school in order to follow two years of cooperative education, there is now a definite advantage to good behavior.

Two institutions are exerting a strong disciplinary influence; two sets of supervisors are applying a code of ethics and behavior. And together the home, school personnel, and job supervisor are asking these 14- 15-, and 16-year-olds to begin to govern themselves.

Again, as schools are run democratically instead of as pseudo military dictatorships, students will feel more of a commitment not only to policing themselves, but to making sure that those they elect to be senators are those who understand the needs of that student body.

Further, with two years of national service following ten years of compulsory schooling, and with a good many 16- to 26-year-olds choosing to do that service in a school setting, youngsters would have a much clearer vision of what it is to grow up in the United States. Of what it means to become a full citizen of a democracy.

Discipline & Counseling

With only a small portion of today's high school students set firmly in a college-preparatory program, and only a tiny portion alternating work assignments with academic classes, a huge mass are left to take "general studies" leading apparently nowhere; it is small wonder Gallup finds discipline high on the list of concerns for parents as well as for those taxpayers (some 75 percent) who do not have children in school.

We're no longer an agricultural society, and we're fast moving out of an industrial concentration to a complex economy based on service and technology.

We do our youngsters an enormous disservice by not preparing them for both a technological revolution and a work force centered in service occupations. One learns service by serving; hence the reason for co-op ed to close out the school years for those not immediately college-bound.

And hence the reason for two years of national service, with two years in the armed forces as, undoubtedly, the most favored choice. Particularly if GI Bill-type college payments are a promised incentive for those who double their time; that is, for those who, after their compulsory two years of national service elect to stay on in the armed forces for at least two more years.

Counselors and counseling have a lot to do with how disciplined a student body is—or is not. This is particularly true for those youngsters whose families are not aware of or willing or able to explore a wide range of alternatives.

Clearly, if 14-year-olds are going to have to find cooperative jobs (with two students filling one job slot), and with the job directly related to the skill training in school, then counselors are essential to coordinate this activity.

It will take one counselor for every 30 to 40 students to handle job assignments and related classroom activities.

Youngsters wanting to go to college when only 14 or 15 need a great deal of help choosing among alternatives acceptable to their families. Counselors will need to know, intimately, all the post-secondary institutions within commuting distance of the school district, and to be in touch with some of the more selective institutions with boarding departments.

But there will need to be a whole new cadre of counselors in the building if the schools are to be the centers coordinating national service for young adults aged 16 to 26. These counselors will need to be brokers. They must not only know the young adult, but family circumstances; and know the alternatives for service.

It is they who must keep track of these mobile young people, seeing that none slip through the net. There is already a process in place for finding all such young adults—the Selective Service Program. Using social security numbers for identification purposes, schools will need to be hooked into the national data bank.

It should be possible, for example, for the 24-year-old when she finishes law school in Oklahoma, but who completed high school in Burlington, VT, to go to the school district nearest her in Oklahoma, and get the necessary counseling to choose two years of appropriate service.

Take the lad from the welfare home who "never was asked nothing he knew," and presume that he was counseled to spend his last two years in school alternating between the classroom and a job.

Discipline & Change

We'll have him entering school at four, not in September, but after someone from the school has gone to his home and talked with parents and guardians about when they think he would be ready.

Because he doesn't have many learning toys in his

home, and his speech pattern is beginning to get set in poor speech habits, and because he has a lively curiosity, the school decides he should start in the middle of the winter just after his fourth birthday.

He's placed in a room where he is the only rank beginner accepted that month; where he's surrounded by children aged four, five, and six who are eager to help him with both the 3 Rs and with dancing and drawing.

Following him along through the grades, we find that the teachers keep pairing him with students who can complement his skills. He's not only given breakfast each morning, but his schedule is always arranged so that homework can be done during school hours, before the late bus home. It becomes clear from the way he handles school chores that he'll want to get into distributive education; that is, into a program to teach him basic merchandising.

Even before he reaches his 14th birthday, the school is looking for a store in which he can start to work. Because his family can provide no transportation, one is found on the regular bus route, and he's "hired" (no pay for the first year) to clean up and to learn how to stock shelves as well as to carry bags out to the parking lot.

For the next two years, his school program reflects his need to know how to handle merchandising in a grocery store.

He is paired with another lad who works mornings, while our student goes to school mornings and works afternoons.

During these two years, a great deal of his academic program, which formerly was classical in nature, is now practical. He's learning how to care for his health, how to shop, how to file taxes, how to invest money.

When he reaches his 16th birthday, he's got some choices to make. He can continue with the job at the store (presuming they are willing to hire him), get another job, go to college if this is a desired option, or sign up for his two years of national service.

Again, since we're deciding for him, we'll have him sign

up for the armed forces—particularly the Army and have him request to be placed in the materials division. We'll assume he does a good job, and further that the Army is pleased with his organizational abilities and asks him to stay on for two more years. That is, until he's 20.

He accepts this offer, and at 20 comes out of the Army guaranteed tuition at the college of his choice for as many months as he served beyond the compulsory two-year stretch. What a difference from today's dropout living on welfare payments.

Our present school setup places too many children and too few adults in one large (generally too large) building. By providing under the same roof for other social and civic agencies, each school building would have a flow of adults in and out. By encouraging aides, by hiring teachers on a part-time basis (hence making use of the many classically educated housewives and househusbands who can't work away from home full time), by inviting elders in the neighborhood to spend a little time each day with students, by securing a mentor for each student whose family has not provided one, and by being the agency to oversee national service assignments, the school would not only be full of adults, but full of children who knew why they were there and why they needed the basics to prepare for adulthood.

Discipline & Curriculum

Mortimer Adler's Paideia proposal, unfortunately getting short shrift from those who presently staff our schools, is on to a very important point. And following his script would eliminate an enormous number of discipline problems. His suggestions for how and what to teach for ten years aren't offered as a discipline-problem cure, but they would not only improve teaching, but improve school behavior.

To oversimplify: He calls for eliminating from the basic first ten years of school everything which isn't academically sound and classically oriented. Yes, he would include music, art, dance, drama—and he would emphasize reading (literature), writing (practicing the same exercise over and over), and arithmetic (the true new math from a conceptual standpoint).

Further, Adler calls for less didactic teaching, and more coaching and use of Socratic-like dialogue. Several recent studies have turned up the fact that in classroom after classroom children are sitting passively (often it's those too smart to be passive who are the discipline problems) while an adult is telling, telling, telling; talking, talking, talking.

Discipline problems in school, while they are, of course, connected to home controls and discipline, are the fault of the school; that is, each of our schools is responsible for the behavior of those within it. And each of our schools must stop blaming the children because they are failing at the job.

Enormous accommodations are being made today which are creating social dynamite for the future. Thousands of teenagers, many with part-time jobs, "hang around" school, drifting in and out of the parking lot, student lounges, halls, and locker rooms, and seldom attending classes. The alienated 15-year-old is supposed to be in school, and so he or she may go there. If these disaffected students do go, they do so for social not academic reasons.

You can find some of them sitting in the back of a classroom wearing ear phones and listening to music from their personal recorders. The teacher doesn't tell them to take the earphones off; instead apparently welcomes the fact that they are "in their own world" and not "disturbing my class."

You can find others leaning over cars in the parking lot, or in a nearby park area playing cards and socializing.

You have a tough time trying to tell teachers and principals of junior and senior high schools facing these unmotivated students that it's their very organization that is the cause of the problem. You have a tough time telling teachers who aren't scholars that they should give sound scholarship to pupils instead of lecturing or assigning pages to be read. You have a tough time asking school counselors to care as much about the non-college-bound as they do about the ones on the college-prep track.

Enough of blaming the schools for a lack of discipline within their boundaries.

Discipline & Blame

The blame more rightfully belongs outside the schools; outside the homes. It belongs to the citizens—to the taxpayers. Time was when only a few adults had ever had anything beyond primary schooling, that those who did the teaching in our schools received some measure of respect.

Admittedly, those who work with their hands have often sneered at those who did not, nevertheless, there was often a grudging admiration for those who "knew their books." Yet, time was when the best educated person in town was the school teacher; next came a time when school personnel joined with professionals and were identified as being "college-educated."

But, we've been offering college at a fast and furious pace to all interested; one state (California, here I come!) even made college free to all takers.

Learning to be a teacher, and then a school administrator, have always, though, been considered vocational skills. Would-be teachers, when colleges were first introduced in the United States, didn't have to take the same rigorous classical academics as other college students. And over the past 100 years, that has continued, even where teachers are preparing for secondary school teaching in history or English or math or physics.

On the other hand, a good many teachers have taken very rigorous courses through their college careers, have the same sound background in their chosen fields as the professional editor, historian, mathematician. A good many of those who have chosen to become school administrators not only have a sound academic background, but have taken management courses which are either the same or parallel the work of any business school graduate.

And so what's the problem? Money.

Yes, money and respect. Morale is low. Rewards are few. Public scorn is taking its toll. Almost half the population in the United States has completed high school and gone at least one year to college. In every community are people with advanced degrees.

For generations, the schools have told students that if they were smart and learned their lessons well they would be rich when they grew up. Year after year the charts are portrayed; charts which tie earning levels to years of education. The dropout earns so much; the high school graduate so much more; the two-year college grad a little more; and so on to doctors, lawyers, merchants, and chiefs.

Yet, the professional teacher is not earning more than the hourly-wage earner in a growing number of occupations; in fact, in some, is earning less.

The credibility gap is enormous. And it's not wasted on older teenagers. They want their chance at the Golden Calf of materialism, and they are certainly not going to sit still for those whose learning has not put them in a stronger earning position.

Interestingly enough, while money may be at the root of many of the discipline problems in our schools, just money is not the solution. That is, paying those who presently staff our schools double or triple what they are now getting wouldn't blow the discipline problems away.

But paying high wages to those whose quality of work is exceptional, and compensating at much lower levels those whose skills have them doing more "pupil sitting" than teaching would go a long way toward closing this credibility gap.

Discipline & Business

Managing our school districts as businesses, and with incentives built in to keep costs minimal, would go far toward giving schools a measure of respect in the business community.

But the real problem is the premise that more schooling

should result in more compensation; and the accusation: If you're so smart why aren't you rich?

We'll never provide a very fine service economy if we continue to worship those who only want to maximize their earning potential. The good life is not goods. The good life is doing good.

Good teachers and principals know that—and that's what keeps them going. And for that very reason, their monetary compensation should be greater than it now is.

It's not true that most school budgets are weighted in salaries paid to the teaching staff; the opposite is true. A disproportionate percentage of each school district budget goes for administrative salaries and costs. There is every reason for the taxpaying public to stop hiring and requiring education-credit degreed and certificated personnel to run the business end of public schools and every reason to put businessmen and women into these slots.

If a school district with at least 10,000 pupils had to split 80 percent for teaching salaries and 20 percent for administrative and all other costs, and the total was not altered down, and if the amount was distributed evenly over all teaching staff, possibly every salary would double.

I know that what you just read is receiving enormous scepticism. But I'm sorry, it's true.

The myth is that teaching salaries are 80 or even 85 percent of all school district budgets. But, sadly, that's true in a very few districts, most of which have fewer than 1,000 pupils. It's not true in most districts; probably not true in yours. But further discussion of ways to improve budgets belongs in Chapter Six.

Discipline & Variety

There's another way to improve behavior while students are in our schools. Somehow, we've done a very poor job of arranging a school day for each of the age groups. There's really not enough variety of activity for our youngest children, and often not nearly enough food served throughout a school day for older youngsters.

Student-run snack bars; maintained vending machines; lunch offerings with a wide choice of popular items; a place to eat a bag brunch, lunch, or snack—these are essential.

Abuse of the area? Closed for the following two school days. Who's to police the area? Students.

As for activity, somehow kids should be allowed to vary their physical and mental activities more often and more informally. Nothing wrong with placing ping pong tables in empty spaces throughout a school building; nothing wrong with letting students shoot baskets during free moments; nothing wrong with arranging for "pick-up" volleyball games on indoor and outdoor courts.

And nothing wrong at all, as has been expressed earlier, in letting a school day start with dancing. No reason not to have a room and recording equipment available for dancing in between classes or for those with free time.

There's no doubt about it; the school day is going to get longer not shorter. We've become a society which is organized around working parents; hence children will be institutionalized during the length of the work day.

Unless the institutions governing children vary their style and pace, the number of kids who are discipline problems will escalate not decrease. Unless we're very careful, we'll make the schools more militaristic, not less. Discipline problems will increase, not disappear.

The choice is ours. But those with simple solutions to discipline problems, for example, suspension from school, wreak havoc when the unruly child becomes the errant adult.

There are thousands and thousands of blacks, poor whites, and Hispanics all across this nation who are between the ages of 16 and 26 who have:

(1) never held a job for as long as a year;

(2) never completed high school;

(3) never scored over the 50th percentile in basic skill knowledge;

(4) have no legitimate source of income;

(5) have the same physical and material needs (as well

as aspirations) as every other 16- to 26-year-old who has a job, has completed high school, and has a steady income. "Social dynamite."

The time and place to defuse that dynamite is during the compulsory school years. Basic skills and basic feelings about participating in our democracy—that's the task of our schools. And we'd better find the best people in town to work with our youngsters; and we'd better pay them well for this work. It costs an awful lot more to institutionalize an adult than it does a child.

Checklist

1. *Cooperation* instead of competition
2. *Democracy* not autocracy
3. *Consensus* instead of intimidation
4. *Rewards* for all, not just a few
5. *Drama* for the "troubled" as well as the achievers
6. *Pairs* instead of working alone
7. *Variety* instead of stultifying routine
8. *Alternatives* instead of a single syllabus
9. *Contracts* instead of edicts
10. *Co-op ed* instead of vocational training
11. *Counseling* not preaching
12. *Coaching* instead of lecturing
13. *Merit pay* not single-salary schedules

Parents: You are the key to the dramatic changes needed for our schools to become less competitive, more democratic, joyous, healthy, productive environments. Every school authority will need your support to institute the changes called for in this chapter. The above checklist provides you with a gauge so you can determine for yourselves how well your school is doing.

School board members and trustees: Hold your building principals accountable for carrying out numbers 1–7; 9; 11–12 in this checklist. Hold yourselves accountable for numbers 8, 10, and 13. Not only a change of program is necessary, but a change of heart. Our children deserve better schooling than they have been getting; first and foremost, though, they deserve better treatment—more cooperation, more rewards, more alternatives, more counseling, more coaching.

Principals and teachers: This checklist is focused particularly on you, your behavior, your choices, your strategies, your determination, your expertise. You may have always wanted your school to be more democratic and to offer more variety, but felt you were locked in by custom, school boards, and parents. Use this checklist to open a dialogue with parents and school board members; see if the way now isn't open for you to make dynamic improvements.

Improving the Curriculum

By A. Graham Down

Executive Director, Council for Basic Education
Washington, D.C.

There is probably no word which has suffered more abuse than the word "curriculum." As its roots suggest, a curriculum should be ordered, not disjointed; sequential, not discursive. yet the fact remains, as Miss Parsons suggests, that under the guise of options for all, we have allowed ourselves to dilute the force of a basic curriculum with courses like sex education and driver education, which may be better covered outside rather than inside a school, or with flaccid electives, or with more goals than can possibly be accomplished in 180 school days per year.

As the Council for Basic Education has said in its Model Curriculum, a sound curriculum should have unity, coherence, and flexibility. A good curriculum should challenge all students not some, and should proceed with gradually increasing complexity, difficulty, and requirements. Around 85–90 percent of elementary schooling should be spent on the basic subjects making up the liberal arts curriculum, and as this percentage lessens in high school, electives should be equally rigorous and challenging.

It goes without saying, however, that an improved curriculum cannot be effective without a parallel improvement in teaching practice. For years we have tended to assume that teaching and talking are synonymous. While we coach for athletic skills, we rarely recognize that coaching is appropriate particularly for mastery of the learning skills in the elementary grades. Perhaps even harder to achieve is the Socratic method of instruction essential for students to learn to think critically and independently. Students need to have an emotional investment and intellectual involvement in classroom procedures. Otherwise, they lapse into inertia and little is learned because the teacher is doing all the work.

In fine, if academic standards are to rise, all teachers need to approach their tasks more rigorously, requiring more both of themselves and their students. If schools were organized to achieve this, the future would indeed be propitious for American education.

Chapter Five

Improving the Curriculum

We're in a real downward spiral right now; a kind of chicken and egg phenomenon. Most of the textbooks used in the primary and elementary grades drag out the teaching of the 3 Rs almost beyond recognition. Yet, most of the teachers argue that for the slow pupil, the pace is still too fast.

Further, most teachers don't just teach the arithmetic they know and love, but use whatever text has been purchased to lead the way, not only with what is introduced in what order, but in what way.

Arithmetic should be taught conceptually—most particularly in the first four or five years of school to build a foundation for algebra, geometry, and the use of computers. The time to teach applied arithmetic is toward the close of the high school years, when students must learn to figure percentages, to make out tax forms, to do simple bookkeeping, to understand interest costs, borrowing, investing, and so forth.

But conceptual math, just as good theater, can't be spelled out; it has to be experienced. The text of the play can be spelled out, stage directions can be spelled out, but how to interpret the parts, how to say the lines, how to create the desired feeling—ah, that has to be in the heart, in the soul, in one's way of thinking.

The whole nation, in the late '50s and '60s, flirted with a dramatic change in the way both math and arithmetic were taught. A mighty effort was made to replace rote learning with conceptual thinking.

Dubbed the "new" math, it had an inglorious career. It seems that only 20,000 of the more than two million basic skills teachers were able to understand numerical relationships well enough to be able to close the textbook and to teach out of their own reservoirs.

Teachers who were textbook dependent "freaked out," and asked for text material to do the conceptualizing. Great mathematicians tried—they really did. And the textbook companies tried, too.

Since they couldn't really conceptualize, they switched the order in which they presented new math. Instead of first stating a rule governing numerical relationships and then giving examples, they put the examples first so that the textbook user could "discover" the rule.

It was a treasure hunt without a treasure.

But, if we're ever to improve schools and schooling, we've got to be able to improve or replace some two million teachers and not only what they teach, but the way they teach!

I've chosen arithmetic (math) to start this discussion, but writing and reading, too, need quite different treatment from what they have traditionally been given.

A great many teachers who would never ever play math games, do read and love childrens' books; do read aloud to young pupils; do let their pupils play with the ideas in the books they're reading; do let them make little plays out of their imaginations; do let them write their own or dictate stories which are pure imagination; do encourage dreams and dreaming and the use of words to bring joy or sorrow.

Even the standardized textbooks used for helping to teach reading can be creative, exciting, demanding, and urge a play with words to create feelings. Most of them, though, are not like this, I hasten to add.

Too Little Too Slowly

Instead, like the teaching of arithmetic in standardized texts, every little step in some contrived story is spelled out in detail, and just a few words are introduced in one book, a few more added in another book, a few more in the next, and so forth—as though children met words in such a linear way in their lives.

A good many of the dogs and cats in this world have not been given four-letter phonetic names (Spot or Dash). Children live in towns like Schenectady and La Jolla and Idyllwild. They have names like Hayden, Heather, Horatio, and even Cynthia.

Of course a four-year-old can learn to spell his/her name; the name of the town in which he/she lives. Can learn to read and recognize such a name. Can even evoke a wide range of feelings just seeing, hearing, or saying such a name.

Fortunately, authors do get their books of stories and poems into nearly every home in the nation, into every free public library in the land, and lately even into most of the public schools in this nation.

Did you know that, while almost every suburban primary and elementary public school has managed to have a library with books, magazines, music, and films chosen particularly to interest children, nearly all city and rural public schools have gone without libraries? What books there were in those schools, other than the standardized texts, were brought in by interested teachers and pupils, and had no "home" other than a single shelf watched over by a teacher.

Yet, even when teachers had no library facilities in their buildings, they generally encouraged children to bring library books to school; incredible as it is to write (more incredible to have taught in a school with such a rule), there are still some schools across this land which do not want children to bring their "own" books to school; do not allow pupils to read these books during the school day; and insist that no matter how well a pupil reads, she or he must be in a reading group using the same text as all others, and may not, during school hours, explore in books of her/his choice.

As for writing, the curriculum is somewhat as fixed, and the problem is as with conceptual math. The teacher who is going to teach children to write has to know how to write. The teacher who is going to guide children in exploring the world of numbers has got to be able to conceptualize with related space and numbers.

And, again, texts cannot teach writing. They can suggest, guide, point out rules—much like the driver's manual we all study before taking that all-important driving test. But the text on how to drive a car cannot teach you how to drive a car. You have to drive. And with experience, you learn not only how to judge distances, but how to manage the machine you're driving.

The same with words. You have to try them out. See if they will say and do what you want them to. See if they tell others what you want them to tell. Right now, of course, I'm wondering if my writing is persuading you; if it's interesting you; if you'll keep reading!

A great many children would learn how to read and how to write if they were to use music as one source of ideas; as one source of words and phrases.

The folk dance coupled with a folk song would be a wonderful way to get to know some strong and interesting words. "I'm a little tea pot, short and stout, tip me up and pour me out." Use a few dance steps and a wee bit of acting.

No reason not to start weaving a story about that tea pot. How was it made? What was it made of? How in the world could we find out how to measure the size of a tea pot?

What about pouring problems? Dripping?

Why stout? Are there tea pots which aren't? How come coffee pots aren't the same shape as tea pots?

To get answers to those questions, particularly for children too little for chemistry texts and encyclopedias, there are adults at home and in the neighborhood who might have some answers (right or wrong). An older pupil who loves to tutor younger kids might help find out something interesting about tea pots.

Then, too, the whole class might try making up a story about a tea pot, how it could sing and how it talked to the cups and saucers and what they said about the people who used them.

The poor primary teacher who is told she/he must show

pupils how to find the volume of any size tea pot as an arithmetic lesson might just take his/her case to their union chief. Relax. You can find the volume by filling the pot and then pouring the contents into pre-sized measuring cups.

But I digress, and I apologize. I'm supposed to be talking about improving the curriculum and not trying to get you to use one of my favorite songs in imaginative ways to help you teach the 3 Rs.

Bother September!

Let's explore for a bit just why we might have arranged in the United States for pupils not to enter school when they were ready for school, but to wait until September (or late August south of the Mason-Dixon line).

Someone (I can't discover who the pedagogist was; I have met the man who determined for a nation that school buses would be yellow since in his area police cars were white and fire engines red) someone must have decided that an orderly way to proceed would be to fill classrooms with children who might not be the same age (allowing for up to an 18-month spread), or have the same maturity with school-related activities, but who would have one thing forcefully in common: Their first day in the regular public school would be the first day for every other first grader.

I don't think it was the same person (or persons), but some group of persuasive pedagogists determined that since the children who arrived in grade one would all be at such different states and stages of growth, development, interest, reading readiness—and have had such a varied preschool experience—the way to handle that peculiar situation was to provide each child with the same text— the same reader, the same speller, the same number book, the same music book.

Never mind that 3 out of the 35 had been taking piano lessons for two years; that 15 of the 35 had attended some nursery school; that more than 10 had toy boxes at home full of learning equipment and two older brothers or sisters who had played "school" with them for the past four years; that the remainder had had almost no "readiness" training or experience, few toys, working parents, and little opportunity to be read to out of good literature.

Instead of organizing beginning school experiences at the level of the pupils, someone decided to organize around identical text material. Primer No. 1—that primer would be the primer for every child, until it was determined that a child was ready for Primer No. 2.

Of course, this organizational rigidity so flew in the face of true pedagogy and everything any good teacher knows about ways to motivate and interest children that enormous efforts have been made to work around this fixed pattern. Hence reading groups were born. Of course, it wasn't hard at all for teachers—even those who don't read anything more sophisticated than a condensed book a la *Reader's Digest*—it wasn't hard for them to discover that some of their pupils read well even before entering school and some did not.

And further, that reading over and over and over again simple vocabulary-controlled booklets was actually frustrating, instead of helping, those ready to read. And so reading groups were formed.

But, incredibly, most teachers have confined reading in school to the texts bought by the district; they have not permitted children to read trade books while in the classroom; they have not used these books to help with the teaching of reading; they have not let children read together from one of those books.

They have, to their credit, encouraged children to get such books out of town and school libraries, to report on them during show and tell, and been glad to know they are in the home.

Rote's Not Right

The same pattern, with even less inspiration, has been carried out in the other basic school subjects. Take music— regardless of how much music a child knows when he or she enters school, the music lessons generally ignore this wide range of musical maturity and ability, and this forces a teacher to teach by rote.

And this rote teaching has a deadening effect on all those not privileged to have homes filled with good music, and severely strains the credulity of the children who do come from musical homes and private lessons. That is, it's good for no one.

It's the very rare school which thinks to break children up into arithmetic groups, recognizing the enormous differences in math abilities between children whose preschool experience was filled with number and space concepts and those who learned little more than how to count to ten.

Again, the solution has been to use a set of books that introduces number activities sequentially in the most tedious manner and with little regard to the need to build on conceptual understanding and not on rote memorization of addition and multiplication "facts."

Who in the world determined that schooling should be a class action and not personalized?

And why in the world have most of the educators in colleges and universities (particularly those who prepare teachers for elementary and secondary schools) agreed to teach new teachers to teach in classrooms and schools organized around the calendar and not around human development?

Testing for School Readiness

It was late summer. The young mother (no longer living with her common-law husband in order to spare the children from his abuse when drunk) moved out of the trailer on the back road and into a sparsely furnished old farmhouse with the children's great-grandmother, an uncle on furlough from a mental hospital, and assorted relatives.

Her town offered a special school program for four-year-olds, and her little boy was just four. He was a wild little rascal, had pretty much shifted for himself around adults who had their own problems and saw to it he was fed and sheltered, but not much more.

The mother asked a college-educated neighbor if she and the two children could ride into town with her so that the little boy could be tested by the school. It seems that not every four-year-old who wanted the program could have it. School officials insisted on a visit with the child and one or both parents; they questioned child and parent together and then the child alone. Generally this was done by one of the primary-grade teachers or by the school psychologist.

As they drove the seven miles to the school, the neighbor said to the boy: "You are going to be asked what your name is. So, let's pretend I'm the lady at school. What's your name?"

He got that one in a snap, sat up and looked interested.

She then said: "They'll ask you your mother's name . . ." and before she could go further, he supplied that.

She was more cautious with the next one, talking as much to the 20-year-old mother as to the lad: "What's your father's name?"

He slumped back down in the seat; his mother said, "You tell them you don't know." He glared at her and said, "Yes I do."

The neighbor hesitated for a moment and then urged the mother to let him give the father's first name if asked. They argued for a moment, and then she told him he could do what he wanted.

To get off that dangerous ground, the driver then said: "You're wearing a bright red sweater, and the teacher may ask you what color it is. So, you can tell her it's red."

He smiled at that, and the rest of the trip was silent except for the three-year-old chattering about how she wanted to go to school, too.

The neighbor waited in the car with the baby sister and watched as another mother and her daughter came out, obviously having just completed the test.

Daughter (skipping while holding mommie's hand): "She asked me what color my dress was and I told her it was red and green plaid and she said I was a bright little girl to know about plaid and I told her you had a plaid skirt just like mine but you didn't wear it today and she said did I know my telephone number and I told her I did and that I called my grammy every single morning and that I was going to call her after my test and tell her if I passed and then she said I was certainly ready for school."

It wasn't ten minutes later that the mother and son came back out to their neighbor's car. No skipping. A grim expression on the mother's face. So grim that before she reached the car the three-year-old was whimpering.

Silence for the first five minutes.

Then the mother spoke up: "They asked him where he lived and he said he didn't know. I tried to explain about the trailer up north that we had left and the trailer on the back road with my brother and sister and that we were now in the farmhouse. . . ."

More silence.

Then the lad spoke up. "Jeesum! You was right. She asked me what color my sweater was."

The driver asked about his answer.

"I couldn't remember, so I said: 'Oh s—t, I don't know; but the lady what brought me, she knows.' "

Which child needed help from the town to get ready for grade one? Which child, if not helped by the town with basic skills readiness, would surely fall behind, either dropping out mentally before physically doing so or becoming a discipline problem?

Did the testing teacher really know which of the two needed a preschool experience? Did the testing teacher know the kinds of questions to ask to determine whether a child was getting at home what he or she needed to be prepared for 10 to 12 years of academic study?

Of course the testing teacher knew what she was doing—so why did she offer the four-year-old with the plaid dress and the academically oriented home an extra year in school and deny that training at school for the four-year-old whose home could not provide the correct education?

Family Grouping Not Self-Contained

Now, let's imagine it's two years later and both children are six years old. And they enter the first grade together.

In a family-grouping situation, you have the plaid dress helping the red sweater.

In the self-contained graded classroom, you have the plaid dress in one reading group and the red sweater in another. And you have them together for most of the rest of the school day, causing the red sweater to spend a great deal of time with his face to the wall or in the principal's office and the plaid dress asked to give out milk at recess and to clap the erasers at the close of the school day.

If you've got a heart—and I suppose you do if you're still reading this book—you'll want to know what the mother of the red sweater did.

She moved to yet another trailer in another school district; in one that welcomed her little boy (saying that they wanted to get him ready for school) and offered to take the little girl for half a day (and they provided transportation since she had no car) to get her ready to get ready as well.

Giving each child in school the same lesson or the same book is not fair, is not an example of equity, is not even "sameness," since the children aren't the same.

The curriculum for the first three or four years of school should contain art history, music appreciation, poetry, design, painting, singing, dancing, gymnastics, games using balls, reading, games without balls, writing/spelling, story-telling, non-competitive games, geometry, nature study, counting, history, competitive games, puppetry, clowning, applied research, arithmetic, crafts, board games using strategy, use of calculators and computers. And lessons in the concepts of democracy—particularly in how the United States carries out (or tries to carry out) the principle that each citizen has equal rights.

Do You Learn Visually, Orally, or Kinesthetically?

If you (this is addressed to the reader, and is not as much of a digression as it may seem at this point) had to look up a phone number and the phone book was chained to the wall on one side of the room and the phone was on the other side, what would you do to remember the number between the time you looked it up and you dialed it?

If you could just look in the book, see the number, picture the numerals in order in thought, walk across the room to the phone, and silently dial the number correctly, then we can conclude you are a visual learner. That is, you learn by translating pictures, and you probably have a photographic memory.

If, on the other hand, after you had read the number in the phone book, you walked the short distance saying the numbers to yourself, either out loud, or mumbling in your throat, and as you began the dialing process you continued talking your way through this new number, perhaps partially seeing it as you're saying it, we can conclude you are an oral learner. The same type of oral learner, who, when someone gives you directions to get to the state park, you repeat the directions back to the person who told them to you.

Or, different yet, if you didn't think you could remember the picture of the number, and you didn't trust yourself to say the numerals across the room, you could write them down. If you didn't have anything to write with, you'd probably press them onto your arm or other hand with one finger, getting a feel of how the numerals flow in that particular phone number. That's what kinesthetic learners do.

Now, you who prefer writing the numbers down, can you write them, then not look again at the slip of paper when you get to the phone and dial? Are you the type, if you write out a grocery list and leave it on the refrigerator under the Snoopy magnet, you can still remember most of the items on it; but if the list was written by someone else you can't?

Those who write the number down are kinesthetic learners. A lot of little boys, who have been using toys which require touching and manipulating and maneuvering and taking apart and putting back together arrive at school essentially kinesthetic.

Of course, we all have a mix. We can picture some things, we talk our way through others, and many of us want hands-on experience during the learning phase.

But each of us leans a little more toward one of those three styles of learning: visual, oral, kinesthetic.

And unless teachers and principals know this, and unless they plan the curriculum around this, and unless teachers who are essentially oral learners compensate for this, then many of those who appear to be failures in our schools are really very frustrated learners—as frustrated as we are when we need to remember a phone number and we don't have paper and pencil.

I took a friend to the Franklin Park Zoo in Boston— perhaps one of the worst managed and equipped zoos connected with a major cultural center anywhere in the world. She is a visual learner; first a magazine editor and then a newspaper editor; and plays the violin.

The sign read LLAMA. But in the enclosure were some scruffy-looking burros. "I thought Llamas had long necks," she exclaimed. "They do," I replied. "Those are burros."

"No they're not. The sign says llamas."

Our conversation followed that pattern for a couple more turns around what we were seeing; she left that section of the zoo unconvinced by my arguments to the contrary.

She's a superb proofreader. She spots typos at a glance. She's not at all good at hanging a picture. And she did very very well in school.

Most visual learners do well in school. The curriculum is "stacked" in their favor. Teachers like working with pupils who remember what they see; particularly teachers who aren't teaching concepts, but systems and patterns.

A great many teachers, because they were visual learners and hence did well in school, chose teaching as a profession largely because they had done well and thrived on the praise heaped their way. But many make poor teachers because they don't know enough about how oral and kinesthetic learners learn to be able to adapt the curriculum to their needs.

Spelling is one of the most obvious cases in point. Almost all spelling texts are based on rote memorization. The very choice of words has little to do with orthography and everything to do with visual cues. The names of the days of the week, for example, will be given in one spelling lesson.

But Monday and Sunday (to say nothing of Wednesday) have no rationale for being in the same spelling lesson unless every pupil in a class is a visual learner. And I believe I can safely say that there aren't more than ten class groups anywhere in the United States filled solely with visual learners.

To teach spelling to kinesthetic and oral learners, you need to build words orthographically; at the very least, you must let pupils write out those words under the guidance of one who spells correctly so that bad habits don't get ingrained.

There is a new learning device flowing into our schools which may just make learning how to spell less of a mystery to a good 50 percent of the population. The computer! Computers, some of them, that is, contain spelling teachers who are patience itself. And they combine all three learning styles. You've got to do the writing (hitting the keys) and most of the time you can say the letters or full word as you go along, and there they are on the screen so that oral, kinesthetic, and visual learners are all accommodated.

In the meantime, teachers are going to have to recognize the need to offer all the material they teach to all types of learners.

Gains From Peer Teaching

Probably the reason pupils who are having trouble with a basic skill learn more by teaching than by being taught is that they must talk things out to learn them, and this they get to do when teaching another. And the one who needs hands-on or writing, will use these to teach another, and so use the very technique so fundamental to his progress.

Further, it is generally the kinesthetic who need the tutoring and generally it is the kinesthetic who are chosen to do the tutoring . . . why? Because most visual learners don't make good tutors. . . .

It's through the curriculum in the first four years in school that these learning styles should be nurtured, and every effort should be made to help the kinesthetic to be more oral and visual; to help the oral with visual as well as kinesthetic skills; and to provide the visual learner with opportunities to develop both oral skills and hands-on knowledge.

At this stage of schooling, art is as important as reading. Drawing is as important as penmanship. Geometry is as vital as counting. Singing is as compelling an activity as kickball.

And at this period in young students' academic careers, all the curriculum they meet should be integrated. What they study in history and geography should lead them to reading and writing, to determining numerical facts, to using drawing talents, to singing and dancing and role playing.

Even if there were some teachers with as many multiple teaching skills as there are subjects to be taught, even so, it would be well for young children to have several adults each day lead them in their activities—adults who praise, cajole, threaten, and reward them as they grow and develop as students.

Quite the same curriculum needs to be provided whether the pupils start school at age four or at age six. A great deal more drawing will need to precede penmanship for more four-year-olds than six-year-olds, but that's about the only significant difference in the offerings.

Also, teachers of this age group, working out of family groupings, should not be overinterested in preparing pupils for a "next" step; or the next text in the series. Instead, the teaching should be what suits the children as a group and each child as an individual. The child who wants to read "The Gingerbread Man" should be allowed to do so, and possibly even helped to make a figure out of gingerbread.

And the same age child who dotes on poetry might want to read over and over "How the Elephant Got His Trunk," and be interested in building a papier-mâché elephant.

If the whole class gets interested in monarch butterflies in the fall, first finding the milkweed plant and then the correct caterpillar, this need not be confined to the 15 minutes a week pre-scheduled for natural science. This is a grand opportunity to learn how to do some simple research; develop some study skills; widen a vocabulary; learn new spelling words; build a graph plotting time for each stage of development to take place; and so on.

This integrating of all the various basic skills, combined with adapting to the three distinct types of learning styles, builds a solid base for the next three or four years. It's in these middle school years that study skills must be honed, and students must learn how to learn. It's a time, too, to begin to build a broad base of knowledge; a time to read classical literature; a time to develop an appreciation of classical art; a time to strengthen appreciation of folk and classical music.

¿Hablo Usted, Español?

Observation, invention, and study—those are basics for all scientific thinking. The curriculum for these 8- to 12-year-olds should build on the concepts introduced in the primary grades and add on one more—the learning of a second language.

In a growing number of school districts, this language will be Spanish. If for no other reason than the fact that the children who go to school with each other in portions of the Northeast and most of the Southwest as well as Southern California need to know both Spanish and English.

Up until a short time ago, German was the second language spoken by most U.S. citizens. And just a tiny bit of history will explain why it is school principals and teachers have been so retarded about offering foreign language teaching to all pupils.

First came World War I. Prior to that "war to end all wars" with Germany, almost every secondary school across the nation taught German as well as Latin and several other languages. In reaction to that conflict and its destruction of so many of our young men, the teaching of German almost disappeared from the schools.

But gradually German began to regain its popularity; not only was much beautiful literature and music written in that language, but physical scientists found it necessary for understanding many scientific papers.

Then came World War II. What Kaiser Wilhelm started, Adolf Hitler completed. The German language disappeared again, and with those two conflicts came a growing sense that English was the dominant language (that it would be so throughout the world, even replacing French as the language of diplomacy), and that when children came to school speaking anything other than English they should not be reinforced in that bilingualism, but forced out of it while in school.

A great many school teachers 30 and 40 years ago were first-generation Americans as well as first-generation college graduates. Their blue-collar parents wanted them to succeed beyond their "stations" in life. And this included becoming "American." And Americans speak English. Yes, they wear native costumes for parades and schooltime show and tell. But essentially the message slipped across the country—English is our language; Americanized English, that is!

In a great many school districts, to not have at least two languages spoken (as well as taught) at school, seems to be perversity itself.

Told about a school which was supposed to have an excellent bilingual (Spanish/English) program, I arrived at the school after driving around the neighborhood for 15 minutes. Clearly, Hispanics occupied nearly every single home, and store signs were more in Spanish than English. When I was greeted by a Japanese/American bilingual specialist, I began to doubt my informant.

But within moments I recognized that I was in a school full of magic. The Japanese/American was fluent in Spanish and English and spoke with humor and love the barrio Spanish of the children as well as a Mexican blend which was used for teaching.

At that school, and at many others, efforts are made to maintain the first language of a child who must learn English as a second language; just as English is maintained for all for whom that is their first language. But we all need to learn at least one second language. Some of the lessons taught should be taught in that second language, and we should be teaching that language not to satisfy some college requirement, but because an educated man or woman speaks, reads, and writes two languages.

Our schools got caught up in the graded and lockstep approach to education. Grade one prepared for grade two; grade two for three; junior high for senior high; and senior high for college.

If the colleges require three years of one language for entrance, then all high schools offer at least one foreign language. If colleges don't require a second language, then many high schools drop languages from the curriculum.

Why? Every single solitary study of schools and schooling which touches on language teaching and international understanding calls for more language teaching, not less. And that's because we all live together on one grand sphere, and we need to know each other.

Then, too, there is the very study of language itself. By studying another language, we begin to deepen our understanding of how our own language is built; and this helps us to use language more forcefully, poetically, compellingly.

When first we were teaching second languages in our secondary schools, we made the same horrible mistake we've made with the teaching of arithmetic. Just as those who teach arithmetic don't know enough math to teach conceptually, it turns out that those who taught foreign languages didn't know how to speak the language fluently. Once again, textbooks took over. Children studied French listening to the teacher's explanations in English.

We copied from dictation; we translated written paragraphs from one language to another.

And this lead to the tape recorder. Ah, let the local teacher be a language dolt, and let the pupil learn the "proper" accent from a native expert via the language laboratory.

It's positively astounding that any school board member, superintendent, or principal ever hired a language teacher who couldn't first demonstrate fluency in the language(s) to be taught. Just as the young friend of mine was asked what history books he had on his shelf ("none," was the answer), why have not all districts required language proficiency of all language teachers?

If the tape recorder could talk with you, and help you with vocabulary as you chat together, if the tape recorder could sing and dance with you, if it could make jokes you understand and laugh at the ones you're trying to make, then a tape recorder could substitute for a teacher. But recorders have enormously limited teaching use. Probably their best users are language teachers, particularly those teaching a language they do not have an opportunity to speak frequently with one who has an excellent accent.

The computer is going to be an enormous help in language teaching, particularly for written translating exercises.

But language teaching needs a teacher, and as has been suggested over and over in this book, one way to supply teachers is to reach out in the community and find those who speak a second language and welcome them into the lunchroom, classroom, study hall. Find a French-speaking big sister for a girl struggling with French.

Learning to Be a Good Sport

The child who enters one of our schools at 4 should, by the age of 12, have learned to swim, to play ball games, singing games, board games, computer games; studied art history and learned to draw, paint, work with clay, and do several crafts; worked with geometric figures, calculators, graphs, math puzzles, geo boards, and number systems; read poetry, and mysteries, and horse stories, music, plays, stories, books; studied history, at least one second language, natural science, physical science, geography, economics, international affairs, and the concepts as well as the form of democracy. Should have learned to spell, to use a dictionary, how to build vocabulary, to write phrases, sentences, paragraphs, stories, directions, recipes.

Forget football, concentrate on those sports requiring more individual decision-making, more individual skills. Lacrosse, hockey, and soccer as well as all the track and field sports can substitute for this conflict activity.

Children in the United States really could be taught to play field hockey as well as ice hockey, and schools could field both coed and single-sex teams in many sports.

Field days, combining scores for both boys' and girls' competitions, could replace the single game for a favored few. Include several different sports with skill-level team gradations.

If there are to be cheerleaders, twirlers, strutters—let them be both boys and girls. On field days include groups of folk dancers and singers. Let younger children, guided by older ones, do imaginative types of relay races.

Think of ways for the children to succeed by cooperating, not competing.

There is every reason for those who run the park system in a community not only to have their offices located in public schools, but to cooperate with those schools by offering recreation programs which complement the school offerings.

Make sure, too, that games and dancing and singing come throughout the school day, releasing energy for growing bodies, and allowing for quiet moments of study to follow periods of extreme activity. And remember, too, as you develop a curriculum which better suits growing children, to offer food at more frequent intervals. An orange here, a cookie there, a glass of milk next . . . not big meals, but frequent fuel stops are what's needed.

Those final two or three years of schooling, leading either to college or to a work/study program (co-op ed), need to be seriously and classically academic.

Tailoring Homework to Each Pupil

But before moving to this level of curriculum offerings, let me say that homework—very much a part of every school's curriculum—needs some improving.

Not all homes are alike; not all pupils are alike. We all

know and believe that, so why are homework assignments identical?

Why is the ten-year-old who has been reading since the age of four given the same chapter to read that his classmate is given who's still struggling a bit with sentence meaning and vocabulary?

When a teacher has a whole room full of kids and asks them all to open the same book to the same page and to read the same paragraph, this makes a tiny bit of sense. But to treat homework the same way makes none. Homework is a time to individualize learning strategies; and should be based as much on how well a pupil learns on her/his own as on what each home can provide in the way of support.

There is a very bad habit thousands of teachers have gotten into; it's a bit subtle, so many may not recognize what they are doing is so bad. Teacher after teacher introduces a new step in one of the basic skills, and then assigns as homework the drill activities which the teacher expects will reinforce what's just been introduced.

Teachers: Do you recognize this? Remember when you introduced borrowing in double-digit subtraction and sent every child home to do ten subtraction examples using this new skill? (Parents: You, of course, can recall this moment all too well.)

Each time skill steps depend on homework practice, the children with the home help take a giant step ahead of those whose homes do not or cannot provide that help.

Homework shouldn't consist of "new" business, but of "old." Homework should use and reinforce already understood skills, not work on the cutting edge.

Homework should send children into their neighborhoods, into cultural centers, to talk with their elders, to find examples of what they are learning in the community. Of course, one pupil might be asked to read a complete chapter in a book in order to bring some fact to light next day in class; while another might have as an overnight assignment, the plotting of a simple graph, or a report on a talk with a neighbor about how old his apple tree is.

The school I was teaching in was about six blocks uphill

from a wide river. We began studying rivers and what they had in and on them.

First night's homework: Spend 15 minutes ("if you haven't got a watch go where you can see the church clock") watching the river and note down on a piece of paper everything you see on it and bring that data to class tomorrow.

One youngster had on her list "clouds." Isn't that lovely!

A subsequent homework assignment called for her to go to the public library and find a poem about a river or rivers and read it. She could tell us about it if she wanted to the next day, but if she didn't, all she had to do was read it.

Before long, though, she had formed a poetry club in the corner of our schoolroom, and the rest of us had to listen to a lot of watery poems before we got onto chess tournaments.

Somewhere in the middle of our study of the river, I asked rather innocently for someone in the class to tell me whether the river was moving "this way or that." To my astonishment, not one of them thought they knew for sure, and one of them was quite sure it didn't move at all. She was vehement.

"Well," says I the autocrat of a teacher, "what makes you so sure that river doesn't move?" Her answer humbled me considerably.

"My homework last week was to talk to three people who live near the river and to ask them about what they had seen on it. I talked with that old man I told you about and I asked him if the river had always been there and he laughed at me and said: 'course it's been there; been there long before you was born and long before I was, too.' And so that's why I know that river doesn't move."

After we got that straight, we voted on which way the river current moved, and we were split about half and half. Then came the homework assignment: "Find out from someone you know what direction they think the river current flows in, and find out from the same person or another how we could test what we think to find out if it's true."

The class decided that the best way to find out was to throw Willie Mae Wilson in and watch which way she floated since she was deathly afraid of the water and throwing her in would kill her and so she wouldn't have any way to move herself and so we could see, "for sure," which way the current was moving.

Of course, we all went down there in a class group, each with a stick, threw them all in, and decided it moved "this way" and not "that."

Time for the Classics

By the time students complete elementary schooling, their work should have become decidedly classical; at least some of it. Certainly they should have watched, and often taken part in, plays which are scenes from the classics. They should have learned to appreciate not only folk art, but classical art; not only folk music, but classical music; not only modern story books, but classics as well.

And as they approach their eighth, ninth, and tenth years in school, they should be grappling with some of the finest thinkers the world has ever known. For those not going on to a liberal arts college, this may be the only time they are formally introduced to such thinkers and their accomplishments.

This is the time not only to learn, but to learn how to learn, and to learn how to appreciate learning. Role playing, dramatic productions, operetta, simulations, board and computer games all should be active in the curriculum.

This is the time to stretch neophyte thinkers; it is the time to introduce symbolic logic, electric circuitry, drafting skills, graphing, physics, astronomical calculations, economic geography, and to build on the early concepts of democracy by studying court decisions as well as government regulations.

Debate teams, chess tournaments, science fairs, combined sports and dancing field days, one-act plays, light operas, juried art shows, juried music competitions, including chamber as well as orchestra and band, craft fairs, dip lunches, mixed doubles ping pong tournaments, all-school Capture the Flag competitions. These aren't EXTRA curricular! They are essential to the curriculum.

These are the very activities which bring learning alive and which allow for the slowest to keep up with the fastest. It allows for those who undoubtedly are headed for research labs after post-graduate study in a major university to share what they know with the friend who will be serving delicious lunches in the hometown diner for the next 40 years.

It's more than possible that when the two school senators are elected, one will be the future chemist and one will be the future short-order cook. Certainly that's how it works out in our democracy for those people to work together in town councils, school boards, civic projects, legislatures, and to serve together on juries.

Democracy—More Than Civics

Our curriculum today is almost devoid of any teaching about the concepts of democracy and only contains a few lesson on the form; on civics, if you will.

That's not good enough. Interestingly, learning the meanings behind what governs our nation is so complex that most basic history and social studies textbook series give up almost altogether. Oh, yes, they all explain about the three branches of government, and explain voting procedures.

But the "pursuit of happiness" as a fundamental and basic principle of democracy is almost entirely neglected, and it is the very foundation of why we work so very hard in the United States to treat our neighbor as we would ourselves.

"Life, liberty, and the pursuit of happiness." Those are exciting ways to think about our lives, particularly what this means in our pluralistic society. And further, how such grand ideals play out in reality in a nation which was so slow to permit women to vote; and is still adjusting to the fact that blacks hold full citizenship rights.

In a small country school some 30 or so years ago, the

fire bell rang, and at first the pupils (grades five through eight) thought it was just another drill. But suddenly the ceiling in their first-floor classroom began to come down and a light fixture exploded against a high bookcase.

The pupils had lined up the moment they heard the bell, in the prescribed order, which was the bigger children first (they occupied the front desks) and the littler ones last. When that light exploded, the teacher, a tall man, panicked and thrust his way through the line of pupils in order to get outside. He shoved one girl so hard, he broke her arm against the door jam.

My brother, one of the taller ones, and already outside, quickly saw that the last of the line wouldn't get out before the rest of the ceiling fell. He whipped back into the room calling for me and for all the others to dive under the desks. We did so, the ceiling crashed onto the desks; the lights exploded; glass sprayed all over. None of us was hurt.

When I teach a lesson in democracy to primary pupils, I often use this story and I follow by asking two questions.

"The grown-ups came and put the ceiling back up and after three days the pupils went back to school; do you think that teacher came back, too?"

As one, pupils I ask this of always answer, "No."

Then I ask, "Do you think the grown-ups helped that teacher find another job; one that didn't have him being responsible for children?"

The children chorus the same response, a resounding "No." But I go on to explain that the answer is "Yes," and say that's because we're a democracy. That that teacher needed to earn money so he could pay the cost for that little girl's arm to get fixed, that he had a family he needed to support, and that the grown-ups helped him find a job in another town in a hardware store, where he was a good worker.

I explain further that "pursuit of happiness" in a democracy doesn't mean we have to do it all by ourselves, but in conjunction and cooperation with each other.

What I have found interesting is that wherever I've told that story about the fire drill and the naughty teacher, regardless of the socioeconomic group being addressed, the children all give the same response—no, no one helped that teacher. After I explain that they did and why they did and tie it to the U.S. Constitution and the Declaration of Independence, they are very thoughtful and even little six-year-olds make some interestingly profound comments about life and liberty and happiness for all.

The Best Is Best for All

Mortimer Adler, in his Paideia proposal, repeats several times—referring to compulsory schooling—that what's best for the best is best for all. In the suggestions I am making about improving schools, and with the organizational change to start formal instruction at the age of four (or thereabouts) and to end ten years later, I trust you understand I want all children to have the best instruction from the best teachers under the direction of the best principals in the most conducive atmosphere.

I don't mean to change that when the breakpoint comes after the tenth year, but I do believe this is a natural place for some students to go on to a college experience and for others to spend two years in a cooperative education program. Since this book deals only with elementary/secondary schooling and not post-secondary, let me just say that I would expect college-bound youngsters at this age to flow into an enormous variety of two-year and community colleges.

I would also expect that many private secondary schools would now offer boarding places to these 14- and 15-year-olds and prep their students for senior college. It's possible, too, that every school district that can swing it fiscally would establish two-year colleges.

But it's the curriculum for cooperative education students we'll consider here. Since there are only a few secondary schools nationwide which now offer co-op ed, the curriculum for these students is not widely known.

Briefly, a co-op ed student is one who spends part of each day (or a week or even a term) on a job and the other half of his time in school. The job and the schooling are related; that is, if the student is working at a job in a gas station, the schooling supports that experience. Gas station owners and chief operators, almost to a man, say they will train the kids to change tires, grease, replace oil filters and faulty windshield wiper blades, pump gas, etc. And what they want the school to reinforce is promptness, courtesy, thoughtfulness, patience, and so forth.

The kids need to know how to handle money, and since they are getting ready to be employees and "on their own," need to know what that entails regarding banking, insurance, housing, food preparation, etc.

But students who are going to work in gas stations need some physics, some chemistry, accounting and bookkeeping skills; need to learn management and organizational skills, psychology, sociology, and communication skills.

The co-op ed student who shares his time between clerking in a store and attending classes needs to learn many of the same lessons, but wants to learn merchandising as well.

Each co-op ed school would have its own special curriculum needs; and these would be tied in directly with what the community offers in the way of jobs. In this way, local schools would be within their rights to offer a limited curriculum. That is, in downtown Boston, probably there would be no supporting curriculum for farming or agribusiness, but students finding jobs in the high-tech industry, fishing, banking, insurance, publishing, and so forth would need a curriculum to support these work experiences.

As we move to more of a service economy, the curriculum for co-op ed students will have to change to accommodate this. For example, at the moment the few school districts which now offer co-op ed generally do not have a supportive curriculum for the tourist industry, yet it is one of the fastest growing sectors of private business.

Then, too, there are some businesses which unions apparently are unwilling to share with co-op ed students. Students this age, of course, could not drive trucks, but they might be able to learn much about the trucking industry from the sales and service ends, and from serving at truck stops.

Develop Your Own Course Material

All this means that school districts should either have on staff curriculum developers, or hire one for a year to study the market and to develop the complementary course material to support directly the work experiences.

It's possible to combine two jobs to do this curriculum development as an ongoing activity. Hire as a co-op ed guidance counselor a man or woman skilled in curriculum preparation and have them not only locate the jobs, but cooperate with the employers to determine a suitable job experience, but further, develop some of the course material to be taught by the full-time teaching staff.

It's quite possible that some of the secondary-level academic teachers now in place are more than capable of doing such curriculum development. For example, all the teachers of natural and physical science, told what jobs the co-op ed students will be holding a year hence, might be able to develop a curriculum and set of courses to provide just the right academic background to support the work experience.

Teachers who are soundly enough grounded in their disciplines, who have the interest and the devotion to give to such an activity, should, of course, be those who are provided with "merit" raises.

Interestingly, a school building filled with co-op ed students—and filled with a day care center, library, police substation, etc.—should ideally operate year round. These students need a month's vacation, perhaps in the summer for a student working in a ski resort or in the winter for the student clamming off the coast of Maine. But they also need to learn what it is to fill a job full time.

Remember, each job is filled full time by two students. And for the students their "full time" consists of half job and the other half academic study. Two years is a short time to prepare youngsters in their mid teens to cope with both the demands of a job and society's requirements for adulthood in the United States.

Because the students who choose co-op ed would have had the same classical schooling as the college-bound, they might after their two years of combined work and study decide to go immediately to college. They might have learned in that truck stop that they really wanted to become a mechanical engineer and want to attend a technical college, starting off paying the tuition with their meagre savings from their second year of co-op ed.

But what about the student who, at 14, starts college and is either invited to leave or decides to on his or her own? And what about the co-op ed student who decides to switch to college or is rejected by an employer before the two years is up?

If, of course, the co-op ed student isn't "working out" in one job setting, it's incumbent on the school authorities to find one that will work out. Perhaps more supervision is necessary; perhaps the work assignment needs to be in a police setting for supervisory purposes; perhaps the case is so sensitive that the work assignment needs to be within the immediate school setting, and not "outside."

The student who leaves college before age 16 must, of course, come back to school and enter the co-op ed program.

It is not realistic to believe that states would change the requirement for young people to leave a school setting before the age of 16, even though the ten years of elementary/secondary schooling would have ended at age 14. What is interesting is that community and junior colleges abound now across the United States; and that a great many colleges and universities permit students to complete two-year college programs with or without a commitment to a full four-year degree.

That is, we already have in place the college programs necessary if half our high schoolers are going to leave school about the age of 14 and step into a college program. In fact, there are what amounts to many co-op ed programs already in place in hundreds of colleges and universities nationwide. For example, many allied health programs which train men and women to serve as technicians, nurses aides, and medical support personnel combine some on-the-job training with appropriate academic course work.

In order to do a better job of placing students in four-year college programs, in two-year associate degree programs, and in high school-level co-op ed, our secondary schools are going to have to radically improve their guidance and counseling personnel. This will be spelled out in more detail in both the chapter on improving budgets and improving parents.

It can safely be said that almost none of the counseling staff now in place in most high schools has had any experience with co-op ed placements, or apparently know much about the two-year associate degree programs available in so many universities and community colleges.

Not only will this counseling require dramatic changes, but so will the curriculum changes have to be dramatic. There are very few high school-level courses taught today to 11th and 12th graders which have as their goal support of a work experience. That is, the natural science, biology, or botany courses now in place in most high schools, and for the most part textbook oriented, wouldn't be entirely applicable for a mix of co-op ed students training for jobs in greenhouses, on golf courses, at recreation centers, as nature guides, summer camp counselors, and so forth.

What will be necessary is for someone well versed in natural science to put together a strong academic course which complements the work experience. And, as Adler requests in his Paideia proposal, such academics would be a combination primarily of dialogue and coaching and very little lecturing.

A New Comprehensive Secondary School

Following along the lines suggested, we now have what we have all along claimed for our schools—a comprehensive program fitting some for jobs and others for higher education without cutting either out of a second choice.

But what I am recommending does not include—what sadly presently abounds—thousands of students fitting themselves for neither college nor direct employment. They are just going through some rote set of academic assignments which suffer from a weak base, and hence we have the sad picture in the United States of one out of four young adults barely at the level of functional literacy.

They have been enrolled in "general education" courses; despised by themselves, their peers, the faculty, and the community.

And as one more inducement to push for a ten-year academic diet followed by two years of co-op ed for some and college for the others, this will stimulate more field day-type athletic events and fewer varsity team events. It will stimulate, as well, more learning of individual rather than team sports, and of more recreational team activities such as volleyball, water polo, surfing competitions, sailing, skiing, and so forth. We've let athletics dominate us far too long in our junior-senior high schol structure. No reason at all for varsity athletics not to become a community club activity. Let there be sponsors for teams, and competitions set up to suit those who would participate— much like is done now in the several summer baseball leagues.

Children 14–16 who are part time in school and part time on a job have to learn and enjoy athletic activities which fit in with their schedules. They will have to join clubs if they want to play organized sports; the co-op ed secondary school won't be able to accommodate them. This will certainly cause an enormous disruption to the present senior high athletic schedules.

Since many of the students who might otherwise have been in the varsity sports program will now be at a two- or four-year college, and should these colleges want to invest in a heavy varsity sports program, it is there that high school varsity coaches will need to go.

And this will leave in place in the schools, those coaches who love intra-mural sports activities; who love teaching individual sports; who want to combine some athletics with classroom teaching; who love organizing multipurpose field days combining sports, dancing, and singing.

Preparation for Independent Living

What we're going to have to do with the curriculum in these co-op ed schools is teach food preparation and home economics, not for institutional purposes, but to teach our youngsters how to run their own apartments and homes. We're going to have to teach them how to care for cars and houses and yards. How to care for small children and even infants (it will be good to have a day care center located in every school); how to do small electrical and mechanical repairs on service equipment; how to budget funds and time; how to deal with social service agencies, for those in one income bracket, and how to maximize their savings, for those in another income bracket.

We should, of course, be teaching all our older high schoolers how to do all these things now. We're letting thousands of our young people drop out of our schools without getting any practice or advice in how to cope with job/recreation/family/civic responsibilities as an independent adult. Whether we alter school schedules to send our youngsters on to colleges and universities after ten solid years of academics, and whether we offer every student who doesn't go right to college co-op ed, we must alter the curriculum to teach every youngster how to use the democracy of which she/he is a part. How to handle judicial matters, how to participate in the political scene, how to make use of the boards of civil authority, how to vote, how to invest money and time wisely.

Perhaps if all homes were more stable and all communities were the size that all the families knew and cared for each other, then we could argue that schools didn't have any responsibility to teach citizenship skills. But that's not the case, and lessons in participatory democracy are essential.

And now for a quick deletion of curriculum which has gotten into schools and belongs in other civic and social agencies.

Driver education—let the state highway patrol take over that program, now.

Health education—let the state health department offer

volunteer courses during non-school hours to both school-age children and out-of-school adults, to all who wish to participate. These classes, could, of course, be taught in a school building, but they should not be part of the regular school responsibility.

Daily prayers—let all interested homes and Church-supported schools teach that activity to all volunteers.

Sex education—let all interested homes provide whatever instruction is deemed necessary. Let the state health department, as part of their volunteer courses, offer sex education to all interested volunteers.

Religious instruction—let all interested homes and religious bodies prepare whatever they prefer for volunteers during non-school hours.

Now, one final warning about a pernicious danger as our nation (and our world) becomes more and more technological. The danger is that school curriculums will allow only for children to use computers, pushing keys and moving sticks as they follow pre-programmed instructions.

Yet, what's badly needed is for us all to know how to tell the computer what to do, not just to follow the computer's instructions.

Let me make an analogy. We teach music in all our schools, but infuriatingly, most schools only teach rote reading of music. They do not teach children to compose and sing or play their own music. Yet we should learn how to do both.

And so it is with computers. Just as I'm using my computer to program my word-processing package, so I should also learn how to tell the computer how to program word processing to suit my needs.

If one is computer "literate," is it not a fact that such "literacy" implies being able to make the computer do something instead of the user just doing what the computer tells him/her to do?

And so it is with music—to be "literate" in music we need to know how to not only read the notes, but how to compose notes to make music.

And so it is with our reading and writing—to be "literate," we need not only to be able to read and copy what others have written, but to compose thoughts into words ourselves.

And to be "literate" in math, do we not need to puzzle numerical and spacial relationships out for ourselves?

While it may take years to change our school systems over to accommodate the 4–14-year age group and to offer only job training and academics, it should be possible for every school within a calendar year to change the curriculum for the better. Hundreds have. Maybe your neighboring private or public school has already got a curriculum change you're considering.

It's very worthwhile finding out.

Checklist

Good teachers, principals, central office staff, and superintendents are always thinking of ways to improve the curriculum. I freely admit it; many of the suggestions in this chapter on improving the curriculum are programs I've seen in operation in selected spots up, down, and around the United States. Check off those you feel you've already instituted, and note those yet to be implemented. The first 24 don't require enormous outlays of money, nor are they socially or pedagogically complex. They do require enormous outlays of energy, but our children do deserve the best.

* * *

1. Teach arithmetic (and math) conceptually from the earliest grades.

2. Save applied arithmetic (percentages, etc.) for the closing years of high school.

3. Stop being textbook-dependent. Teach out of a rich personal reservoir.

4. Play with words; encourage dreams and dreaming.

5. Give beginning readers stories which are creative, exciting, demanding.

6. Encourage the use of trade books as reading texts.

7. Writing has to be a constant activity.

8. Use music and dancing for story ideas in writing lessons.

9. Teach reading by performing folk music and dances.

10. Integrate all basic lessons. Weave science, arithmetic, penmanship, spelling, singing, drawing, etc., etc., into one lesson.

11. Expect children to ask other adults for help with concepts and ideas brought up in school.

12. Start the curriculum at the level of each beginning student; don't give 30 first graders the same school lessons.

13. Have children create and compose songs—use music as a vehicle of expression; don't just learn songs by rote.

14. Personalize the curriculum; good schooling is not a class action.

15. Reach out to help those whose home situations don't provide much academic support; vary the curriculum to meet their special needs.

16. Arrange the class so that the children don't compete but help each other.

17. In the first four years of school teach: art history, music appreciation, poetry, design, painting, singing, dancing, gymnastics, games using balls, reading, games without balls, writing/spelling, story-telling, non-competitive games, geometry, nature study, counting, history, competitive games, puppetry, clowning, applied research, arithmetic, crafts, use of computers, concepts of democracy.

18. Vary lessons for learners who are visual/oral/kinesthetic.

19. Only a few of us can learn to spell by rote; we need to build words orthographically and have an opportunity to write (not copy) them when learning new words.

20. Spelling via computer helps all learners, regardless of style.

21. The youngest children need drawing experience to precede penmanship lessons.

22.   Since youngest pupils are learning how to learn, singing is as important as kickball; art is as important as reading.

23.   As soon as study skills are learned, apply them to research activities.

24.   Study the classics: literature, art, music.

25.   Teach every child a second language; help maintain a first language for those for whom English is a second language.

26.   Regularly use a second language as the language of instruction.

27.   Study a second language to understand how language is constructed.

28.   Every language teacher must be fluent in the language(s) taught.

29.   Assign language teachers (not pupils) to the language laboratory.

30.   Institute French-only (or whichever language you choose) tables in the lunchrooms; invite older French-speaking adults to eat there.

31.   Get a Spanish speaking (or whichever language you choose) big brother/big sister for a student struggling with a second language.

33.   By the age of 12, every one of our children should have been taught how to swim, play ball games (but not football), play singing games, play board games (strategy), play computer games; studied art history; learned to draw, paint, work with clay, do several crafts, do geometry, use calculators, read and construct graphs, do math puzzles, use geo boards, use number systems; read poetry, read mysteries, read horse stories, read music, read plays, read stories, read books; studied history; read, write, and speak a second language; learned to do natural science experiments, to do physical science experiments; studied geography, economics, international affairs, and the concepts as well as the forms of democracy; learned to build a vocabulary, to write and spell, and to be a democrat.

33.   Teach U.S. children (both boys and girls) to play field hockey and lacrosse.

34. Have field days with multiple age and skill levels competing in games as well as displaying singing and folk dancing skills.

35. Field co-ed soccer, softball, volleyball teams.

36. Cooperate with the local recreation department to provide offerings to enrich the curriculum.

37. Alternate the school day between periods of quiet study and physical activity.

38. Vary homework assignments to fit each individual pupil.

39. Don't use homework to reinforce "new" concepts; use homework to practice "old" skills or to get fresh data through research.

40. Expect children to have help with homework.

41. Give every child a part in a play.

42. See that every child watches a classical play.

43. Students 12, 13, and 14 should grapple with the ideas of great thinkers; role play; be in a variety of dramatic productions; read and study classical literature; be in an operetta; participate in and design simulations; play board and computer games of strategy; study symbolic logic; study electric circuitry; use drafting skills; use astronomical calculations; study economic geography; learn how to graph; study physics; build on early concepts of democracy.

44. Consider the following as part of the curriculum: debate teams, chess tournaments, science fairs, sports and dancing field days, one-act plays, light operas, juried art and music competitions, craft fairs, dip lunches, ping pong tournaments, all-school games of Capture the Flag.

45. Build democracy lessons around the concept of the "pursuit of happiness."

46. Change the curriculum radically after the basic ten years for those in cooperative education programs.

47. Teach students how to handle their own money; how to borrow, bank, insure, loan, save, invest.

48. Teach merchandising to students working in stores; teach them management skills as well.

49. Change science courses to fit the needs of co-op ed

students working in chem labs, gas stations, nuclear plants, sewage disposal centers, landfills, etc.

50.   Build the curriculum to suit the job opportunities; high tech and computer programming in one setting; farm machinery maintenance in another; gourmet cooking in yet another; motel management in another; petroleum-related activities in another; agribusiness in certain sections of the United States.

51.   Build a curriculum around service occupations; include lessons in promptness, orderliness, consistency, loyalty.

52.   Set up a curriculum-development unit in a large school system; hire a curriculum consultant for a fixed assignment in smaller school districts.

53.   Let good teachers get merit pay for creating needed curriculum changes.

54.   Develop a year-round curriculum.

55.   Accept into co-op ed those who fail out of college; switch into college those who qualify and want out of co-op ed.

56.   Guidance counselors need to know what to tell students headed eventually for academic doctor's degrees; what to tell the student headed for a two-year associate degree; what to tell the student headed for a four-year college; and what to tell the student planning for coop ed.

57.   Step away from textbooks and design original courses.

58.   Let those who want varsity sports make this a "club" activity.

59.   Provide co-op ed students with lifetime sports activities such as volleyball, bowling, skiing, jogging, tennis, sailing. . . .

60.   Include in a "how-to" curriculum: how to care for an apartment, fix meals, repair secondhand appliances, fix secondhand cars, get medical assistance, use social service agencies, deal with juvenile authorities, care for infants, budget limited funds, budget precious time, prepare to be a thoughtful voter.

61.   Delete the following from the curriculum: driver

education, health education, saying of daily prayers, sex education, and religious instruction.

62.   Teach not how to hit the keys of a computer or how to move the joy stick; but how to program the computer to do calculations to support each student's fresh and exciting ideas.

Chapter Six
Improving the Budget

A good many of the improvements suggested so far in this book are inexpensive; in fact, there are some which would save money.

For example, once school chores are done by students, and older students supervise the work of younger pupils, fewer adults would be needed for maintenance of school buildings and grounds. Hence, money presently spent for janitors and custodians could either be transferred to another line on the budget, or be used to reduce the total cost, and hence translate to a tax savings for everyone in the school district.

The idea of having only 300 pupils in an elementary school and additional building space rented out to compatible service agencies, also would have an effect on the capital side of the budget. Instead of just school district funds maintaining a building, the cost for same would be spread over several agencies.

And once a school building is filled for nearly a 24-hour day, and has a steady flow of adults in and out, vandalism would decrease, again a direct dollar savings for a line-item budget.

Hiring all new teachers as interns is a direct savings; as is hiring many people on a part-time basis to help out with specific skills or academic disciplines. For $10,000, for example, a high school undoubtedly could find a speaker fluent in a second language who is willing to teach interested students mornings for the 36 weeks of a school year.

Assuming that a regular, certified, full-time language teacher in that school district would be paid $20,000 a year,

178

two half-time teachers could be "bought" for the same amount.

Family grouping in the elementary grades, thus making every pupil both a student and a teacher, eliminates the need for a low teacher/pupil ratio. Instead, the master teacher, who knows how to organize peer teaching could handle more pupils than a teacher locked into a self-contained classroom.

Let's look at the statistics for the last suggestion. Suppose there are 15,000 pupils in a given school district, and the goal has been a ratio of $\frac{1}{25}$. That's 600 teachers. Now, let's assume that 8,000 of these pupils are in the elementary grades, that the school system adopts not only family grouping, but welcomes neighborhood folks in to tutor and play, and establishes a day care center, welfare agency, and local branch of the public library in the building.

Further, half the children come an hour early; the other half stay an hour later in the afternoon so that the teaching of reading can have very low teacher/pupil ratios.

And so, with these improvements in place, we could easily raise the teacher/pupil ratio from $\frac{1}{25}$ to $\frac{1}{30}$. And for 8,000 pupils that would require not 320 full-time teacher equivalents, but only 267. That's a savings of 53 teachers at an average annual salary of $17,000, and that's a whopping $901,000; or nearly a million dollars a year.

Savings From Co-op Ed

Another obvious savings comes with cooperative education; here, as has been explained earlier, half the student body is on the job while the other half is in classes. Clearly, a 500-pupil secondary school, using the old formula of $\frac{1}{25}$, would require 20 teachers minimum; and if the same 500-pupil school was attempting to ready some students for college, some for a vocation, and others just to graduate from high school, it would take many more than 20 teachers to reach those three targets.

But, instead, if all pupils received a strong classical education through the age of 14—from a grand mix of volunteers, aides, interns, national service workers, instructors, and master teachers—the final two years of co-op ed could be handled by a small staff skilled in matching the curriculum and syllabus to the work experiences of the teenagers. In other words, it might be perfectly possible since no more than 250 pupils would ever be in the building at one time, and a great deal of the necessary teaching is being done by the job supervisor(s), to have 10 teachers handling 500 pupils—250 at any one time.

And, if each co-op ed student was allowed to do some tutoring, either of peers or of younger pupils in those areas in which the co-op ed student feels weak, then each student becomes a teacher unto himself; and, as research has proved, those who teach, learn. And those who are taught, learn, too, but not quite as much.

Having youngsters teach each other is not only pedagogically sound, but fiscally prudent.

There's yet another saving with co-op ed. It's on the job that students would learn the necessary skills using up-to-date equipment; hence a co-op ed school would not need, for example, to purchase and maintain expensive automotive, hairdressing, secretarial, and electronic equipment. Nor would the school district have to hire mechanics, business executives, or electrical engineers. Each relevant business has these; each school could concentrate, instead, on appropriate and compatible academic skills.

We might call this "apprentice ed," and by so doing acknowledge how business/industry and the schools could cooperate. By helping themselves (that is, by training potential employees), industry is helping schools.

Savings From Part-time Employees

From the beginning, I have recommended including singing, dancing, and drama throughout the school years. An expensive way to carry out that suggestion is to insist that everyone who teaches dancing and singing and dramatics be a full-time, certified teacher. That a school district commit itself to tenure such employees.

But that's not necessary. A good many who are enormously skilled in dancing, singing, and drama would welcome part-time assignments with school children; and for the children, it would mean access to a wide range of skills and interests, not just a limited few.

The community member willing to put in six weeks of work on an operetta would undoubtedly be delighted to receive $3,000 for this month and a half commitment. Another $3,000 might buy six weeks of contra dancing expertise, and another $3,000 see a choral production through from initiation to several performances throughout the community.

When school superintendents, principals, and members of school boards look for new teachers, either beginning interns or experienced master teachers, they can, of course, set some conditions. They might want to insist on fluency in a second language, be shown that the candidate has a strong background in the arts and humanities; or brings with him or her a proven talent in music, dance, or drama.

A young woman joined the faculty of a small suburban elementary school as soon as she completed college. She had been combining interests in music (principal cello in her secondary school orchestra), varsity sports (field hockey in a tough girls' league), and academics (honors in math). The first day of orchestra rehearsal in her elementary school multi-purpose room she arrived with her cello offering to sit in.

Consternation! Gradually, the music teacher accepted this as altruism and not competition; out of the classroom woodwork came several more adult musicians. Result: More pupils spent more hours practicing more musical instruments. Further result: Better music from highly motivated students drawing a scattered community closer together.

Savings From Elimination of Varsity Sports

Another clear savings for today's overburdened school budget would be to replace heavy emphasis on varsity sports with more cooperative team sports, individual sports, and field days. Ten tall boys dominate many a school system's sports budget winter after winter. First, there's the care of the floor on which these tall boys run, jump, and slide. Then there's the cost of transporting them to rival basketball courts. Winning coaches are costly; scoreboards and cheerleaders dent the budget.

There's almost no justification for varsity football at the secondary school level, and were schools to cut off full-time academic study at the age of 14, and were students to go either to college or to a part-time job, costly varsity sports would undoubtedly be removed from the regular school curriculum, and hence from the budget. Such team sports—as well as many individual sports—would be organized by clubs and community recreation programs.

While saving on those sports, I would not skimp on indoor and outdoor swimming facilities. Every child in this nation should be taught to swim; it's a national disgrace that so many of our children drown for lack of basic knowledge about how to move about in the water. There's no comparable need for every child to know how to kick or throw a ball; death is not the result of such ignorance.

Nor do school districts have to reinvent the swimming wheel; the American Red Cross already has thousands of trained swimming teachers, a superb program for training more, and is more than ready and willing to provide swimming instruction wherever there is water available. Let school districts contract immediately with local chapters of the Red Cross to begin teaching swimming. If, as must be the case in more than half of all school districts across the United States, if there is no pool which belongs to the school system, then arrangements must be made to use what pools or natural waters are available within a school district. For many communities, this will mean required swimming lessons to a certain level of proficiency for every child, with summer swimming lessons necessary since no indoor pool is available locally.

Savings From Volunteers

This book is chock full of suggestions for using volunteers—such as big brothers and sisters, business men and women who serve as mentors, retired folks with much to share, college students with energy to spare and skills to teach. Perhaps a line needs to be added to the budget for a person or persons to be in charge of finding and coordinating these helpers. But with a very small investment for such coordination, enormous savings in full-time equivalent teachers would be realized. Further, the sour teachers who have had to take up non-teaching duties will have left an academic vacuum. The expensive way is to keep hiring full-time tenured teachers to take up the slack for poor full-time teachers.

Of course, this burdens the budget enormously. But opening the school to interested and capable adults—some of whom, admittedly, should be paid at least $15/hr. for their services—would be a savings in both the short and long run.

Perhaps we need a VTA instead of a PTA. Unfortunately, the notion of parents and teachers working together has degenerated woefully. In the first place, of course, parents are the people in every community least likely to have the time and resources to both parent and put in helping time at school. And evidence mounts that in more and more instances both parents are the family breadwinners, holding down jobs during school hours. For single parents, of course, this is necessarily the case.

There are, though, other adults in the community who do have the time and interest to give to the community's children. Some may be parents; some will have been parents; many, like myself, just love children and teaching and learning. A volunteers and teachers association (VTA) might well find more common ground than even a parents and teachers organization to work consistently at improving our schools.

Savings from Merit Pay

Most school budgets are based on single-salary scales for all teachers. There's usually a grid with rows going down (years of service) and columns going across (graduate credits and degrees earned). If the figure in the first box is $10,000 (B.A. and 0 years of teaching), then the figure in the final box (Ed.D. and 20 years of service) is generally two or two and one-half times as large as the salary in the first box.

And the poor teacher is paid the same as the good teacher. There are many arguments used to support this curiously unprofessional remuneration system. One, that one parent wouldn't want his child to be in the hands of a $15,000 teacher while another parent's child had a $20,000 teacher. Yet, that's the case now based solely on years of service and degrees earned.

Another argument states that there is no "fair" way to tell who is a good teacher and who is a poor one, and that any effort to make such a determination would be so politically skewed that those who deserved "more" would not get it.

And still another argument goes that teachers are so underpaid now that every one of them deserves more, so to pay more to some and not all is morally bankrupt.

One way to compensate not only on the basis of years of experience and earned degrees, but on the quality of the teaching, would be to ask that teams of teachers work with blocks of children. Let one or two of these be master teachers, proven experts at reaching the hard-to-teach child. Let at least one be an intern. Let two or three be part-time specialists sharing from a rich reservoir for a few hours a day or for a few weeks a year.

Let's start with $170,000 as a line item in the budget for teachers' salaries. At $17,000 as an average for a teacher, this amount would yield 10 teachers. And with a ratio of 1:30, some 10 teachers would staff a 300-pupil school for children aged 8–12.

But let's spend that $170,000 just a little differently:

2 master teachers @ $30,000	=	60,000
2 experienced teachers @ $20,000	=	40,000
1 intern @ $10,000	=	10,000
4 half-time teachers @ $9,000	=	36,000
3 part-time teachers @ $8,000	=	24,000
Total		$170,000

We now have 12 teachers instead of 10 to serve 300

pupils, or a ratio of 1:25. Also, we have supplied each master teacher with five support staff.

Of course, there could be more than three part-time teachers working 15 hours a week for $15 an hour. There might be three part-timers with certain talents and skills in the classrooms for 12 weeks, then another three for the following 12 weeks, and yet another three for the final 12 weeks.

And while this doesn't mean more than 12 teachers at a time, it does make it possible for the pupils to be exposed to some 18 different teachers during the course of a year.

And should a school with 300 children aged 4 through 10 employ a classical curriculum and want to include the teaching of a second language, and want to be sure that teaching consists not only of exposition, but of coaching and of Socratic dialogues, not only would master teachers be justified in receiving a salary of $30,000, but the part- and half-time teachers would deserve strong compensation for the time they spend both in class and preparing for class.

If we go a step further and recognize that a 300-pupil school needs a head teacher who administers part time and teaches part time (and is aided by clerks and secretaries for all administrative duties), we now have 13 teachers. Add to this volunteer teachers (that is, older pupils) from the local secondary school, and volunteers from the neighborhood, plus one or two students doing their national service in the schools, and we can begin to appreciate just how far $170,000 would go were some of the improvements suggested in this book to be put in place.

You'll remember that the chapter on improving teachers recommended that those teachers who have never taken physics should sign up immediately and take the course given at the local secondary school. Some of those part-timers getting $15/hr. could be used to take that teacher's class while the teacher becomes a pupil.

What's important is that teachers be judged (let teachers, themselves, carry out a peer review approved by the local school board) as to the quality of their work, and let the best receive the most. But also, plan to use the very best teachers at their convenience, and for many of the best, this will mean part- or half-time teaching.

Savings from Fewer Administrators

Since this book advocates 300-pupil schools for younger children and 500-pupil schools for older students, it will come as no surprise to the reader that one enormous savings which should take place is in administrative costs. And no surprise, further, that this book advocates that principals and superintendents not be paid salaries which are tied to the size of the enrollment.

School districts which have indulged in that kind of "bigness" have really flown in the face of all good pedagogy. Mark Hopkin's log be damned!

A school building with 500 pupils, containing compatible social service agencies, each with a manager, hardly needs a superstructure of administrative staff. Yes to a head teacher, yes to a supply clerk, yes to a secretary/bookkeeper.

A school district with 30,000 pupils would need 50 primary/elementary schools and 30 secondary schools. It's quite possible, were the school board to make good judgments about school placements, that transportation costs could be reduced considerably over what's needed today to get two or three thousand students to a single school plant.

Few school districts have much money budgeted for sabbaticals, for sending teachers to workshops, or for holding them. Few districts expect to buy books for teachers to read to improve themselves. Few districts are prepared to pay for teachers to have in-school phones or to compensate teachers for keeping up with pupils from their home phones.

Also, few school districts know how much they are spending on any one program. Instead of knowing how much it costs to teach phonics, or spelling, or algebra, or to support ten tall boys playing varsity basketball, school district business managers just know how much is budgeted for salaries, fringe benefits, equipment, administrative costs, and so forth.

We need to keep program as well as line budgets, and we need to learn how to allocate percentages of time for duties performed. What percentage of the $30,000 teacher's time, for example, is spent supervising playground recess and what percentage of that teacher's time is spent correcting workbooks? And what percentage of the intern's time is spent on similar chores?

We need to know what it costs to teach spelling, and how much more it would cost to be sure that nearly 100 percent of the children in school really learned how to spell. We need to know what it costs to teach reading, to teach basic number meanings as well as what it costs to teach calculus.

If a 300-pupil school is determined that every teacher and every pupil should be bilingual (Spanish/English), what would this cost to carry out? How many teachers would have to be sent back to school to learn Spanish? How many learning materials would be needed in both languages? How many tutors? How long would it take? How can volunteers help? What about part-time aides? And so forth.

The improved budget is the one that ties costs directly to programs, and hence provides adequate information for making good decisions.

While it may be possible to save money on staff (not likely), it's even more possible to save on administrative costs, particularly when budgets are controlled at the school building level. Many school districts impose layer upon layer of administrators, with little to show for the expenditures.

There are some additional expenditures which would seem to be "bottom line" items, neither frills nor excess administrative costs. Each school should carry an annual supply of money for buying original works of art, for commissioning original music compositions, for doing follow-up studies on students in both co-op ed and college, for beautifying the school grounds, for planting vegetable and flower gardens, for purchasing a lake or hill or valley or river property to use for outdoor education programs.

Savings From Cooperation

Competition, as a philosophical basis for operating a school system, is very costly. Cooperation, as a philosophical base, on the other hand, is much less expensive.

Obvious, of course, when one measures the cost differential between varsity and intra-mural sports programs. Immediate savings in uniforms, equipment, maintenance, travel, coaches, etc., etc.

But the whole notion of competition is based on winners and losers—a kind of academic survival of the fittest. One spends the same on all to prove that only a few need what all have been given. Why else, for example, buy 30 identical copies of the same book unless the purpose is for 30 pupils to compete in some way, such as who can remember the most given the same exposure to identical material?

Or, why have XX number of pupils in a biology lab at one time doing the same experiment unless the purpose is competitive, to see who can go the fastest or whatever? The list is long of expenditures to support competitive school philosophies; to support teachers with shallow reservoirs who need texts and workbooks and answer books and annotated teacher's editions and identical books so that no student at any time is in a position to ask about solving a problem for which an answer has not already been supplied.

It would cost considerably less for equipment, texts, and learning materials if cooperation and democracy undergirded the school program. Let our students learn in groups and pairs; let them guide and help each other; let them work through experiments together in science labs; let them share the same sheet music, the same Go board, the same puppets, the same footlights, the same ping pong tables.

Let community groups and clubs develop teams and leagues and competitive contact sports programs; and let the users pay the cost for such athletic events. And let the schools concentrate on individual sports, gamesmanship, field days, dancing, and fitness.

Savings From Fiscal Integrity

What would you do if you knew that one of the teachers in the district was getting two paychecks each pay period. One in the name of a dead cousin; one for himself/herself? Yes, you'd see that that teacher was fired. But would you turn that teacher over to the police and cooperate with the appropriate authorities, seeking not only a verdict of guilty, but fiscal restitution so far as possible?

What would you do if you knew that some of the administrators in your school district were pulling down more than one salary—one for a dead cousin and one for the administrator? Would you prosecute?

What would you do if you knew the principal used the school phone for personal long-distance calls; that he/she used the school car for conducting personal business; that a salesperson had delivered an "extra" piece of carpet to the principal's home?

What would you do if you knew that an administrator, privy to the knowledge of where the next school was to be built, was "silently" in on the purchase of that property and subsequently in on the resale to the school district for a large profit?

What would you do if you knew the head custodian padded the bills for all outside service by carpenters, plumbers, and electricians; put in for overtime he really did not serve; kept a distant flea market supplied with "surplus" tools; and took a percent of the hourly wages paid government-sponsored workers?

I had an appointment with a member of a large-city school board in her office. She was explaining to me how the schools needed more money from the city; how sad it was that salaries had to be so low. While she was talking a custodian delivered a dolly load of boxes full of letterhead paper and envelopes. Samples were pasted on the outside of each box.

Her name was on the stationery, no doubt about that. But so was her logo and campaign identification for a national political campaign. As he unloaded box after box, the custodian muttered: "I'd sure like to tell the taxpayers about this." He waited while she signed for the delivery, charging it all to the school district. As time moved on, it was clear the school district was paying for not only the printing of her campaign literature, but its postage. Also, school department secretaries and clerks were kept busy stuffing the envelopes.

An elementary school principal, conducting a longtime affair with the local school superintendent, claimed to have 33 teachers on the payroll. Only 30 were actual people; 3 were "shadows." Her explanation for three paychecks for $1,250 each month—"I need special learning materials and the curriculum budget is too small, so together we worked things out this way to get the equipment."

An independent audit was unable to find the equipment, the learning materials, or the invoices. Nor was there any record of the funds going into the school's bank account.

In a suburban school district, all lawn-care equipment is rented and serviced by a local rental company. Costs are very high, but the head grounds keeper argues that school district ownership of the same equipment would be even more costly. An investigation into the ownership of the company from which the school district rents the mowers reveals that the head grounds keeper is the actual owner; a son-in-law is the titular owner.

Because so few school districts have engaged independent auditors, and when shortfalls and embezzlement are discovered so seldom prosecute, it is estimated that hundreds of thousands of dollars in school district after school district are not reaching the target population—the children. When investigative reporters have discovered gross misuse of public school funds, it has taken massive publishing efforts to push local officials to do anything more than fire the offender(s).

Why this peculiar reluctance? When public funds are abused by public officials, that's no time for the public to turn the other cheek. It's time for the public to determine if those presumed innocent are not, in fact, guilty.

The school accountant who siphons off funds for personal use is a criminal, and should be treated as one. The transportation officer who accepts kickbacks for awarding certain bus routes should not just be dismissed, but turned over to judicial authorities.

There's just no way of knowing how much of our money, supposed to be supporting our children in school, is diverted to personal use. But one rule of thumb is useful. If more than 30 percent of the total school district budget is allocated for administrative costs, then undoubtedly some poor choices are being made for deployment of instructional dollars, and possibly someone or several someones are stealing from the public till.

Taking the line-item budget, and tracing actual spending by program, by course, by school, by service, by personnel can reveal whether funds are being allocated as those who run the schools really wish they were. This is also a way for the taxpayer to know just why it is that when the enrollment in the school district is going down, the costs continue to rise!

Savings From an External Auditor

But equally important is the external auditor. Each school board needs to set up independent auditing procedures. Good auditors can provide important suggestions for ways to economize; they also can find fraud and waste. It really is a remarkable thing to do: we give ten years of free schooling to every child in our nation. And we do it with local school board members and trustees (the great majority are elected) who are charged not only with keeping the curriculum up to date, but with fiscal responsibility. The school board is at fault if fraud is a hidden "item" in the budget.

Needed: business managers with proven business experience and an M.B.A. from a recognized business school. Small school districts might employ such a business person part time. Large school districts like Los Angeles, New York, and Chicago will need several.

At one time, it was said that the New York City school system had more buildings than Sears Roebuck had stores worldwide. Sears stores were managed by those with business training and experience; New York's schools by principals who may have had little or no business training.

One fast way to improve our schools is to place better trained business executives in charge of the business end of the schools and better trained academicians in charge of the curriculum and syllabus.

Another fast way to improve our schools is to keep better track of where each dollar goes, and to discover how much of each dollar actually can be traced to direct instruction.

Another fast way to improve our schools is to diversify teachers' salaries, and to pay on the basis of three factors, not just two: a combination of quality, length of experience, and degrees earned.

A quick way to insure honesty in school officials is to bring charges against those suspected of dishonesty, to follow up on those charges, to serve notice to all who work in the public schools that public dollars are precious dollars.

A federal official, looking over a computer printout of expenditures over the course of 12 months in a large and complex experiment, had asked for program budgeting; for costs to be directly connected to the experimental programs presently underway.

The school officials had tried to comply, but program budgeting was new to them. They got lost in the trivia of small expenditures for things like wastebaskets, pencils, and learning toys. They tried distributing all costs over programs, but when they were all through they found they couldn't account for several thousand dollars.

No fraud; no chicanery; no criminal activity. The money in the line-item budget was accounted for; it was this program budgeting that was the problem. They decided to name one portion of the program MISCELLANEOUS, and buried the notification of this expenditure some 150 pages into the printout.

The federal official began browsing through the report, disturbed that costs had not been aggregated per program; worried that the accountants and program supervisors weren't understanding the importance of knowing why it was they should make decisions based on fiscal facts and not just on "gut feelings." The printout fell out of her lap. On hands and knees she began refolding it when her eye noted a sum out two columns farther than its neighbors.

The next morning at the budget meeting she had a bright red piece of yarn stuck in the offending page. Before she could say a word, the business manager grinned and said, "How'd you find it?"

Have you dropped your school budget printout lately?

Introduction to Chapter Seven

Improving Parents

By Mildred E. Jones
President, National School Volunteer Program
New York City, New York

Improve parents to improve schools? Cynthia Parsons strongly suggests that improving parents as a course of action will result in the improvement of schools. Parents, the child's first teachers may well be the remedy needed in very large supply, to bring about a change in the nature of schools in America. For, as the prime investor-developer-special interest group, parents have a self-serving need to be met, the well-being of their children. They represent the single identifiable constituency with the will, capacity, and determination to protect their offspring on a continuing and long-term basis. And, given the enormity of the problem we face, perhaps large-scale parental intervention is the simple solution right at hand which is most accessible and easily converted into action.

As we well know, difficult problems often defy being solved because we often search for complex answers; the simple or most direct answers are generally overlooked. So, too, in education we fail to make a thorough examination of the most obvious and readily available resources. We move from crisis to crisis, reform to reform, innovation to innovation, searching for magic antidotes to cure the ills. In looking for answers we consider many factors, the role of the staff, the training of the teachers, length of the school day, the materials we use for instruction, yet we fail to look at roles other "educators" could play if their services were to be enlisted in a constructive and consistent manner. Parents are usually overlooked as educators within the context of "delivering instructional services."

The potential for using the help parents can provide is limitless; in school, at home, and in the community the activated and already child-focused parent could have a salutary effect on the quality of education in our schools. Parents and other individuals eager to assume parental concern are key to the reform of schools.

So we must be imaginative and resourceful in developing a sufficient supply of "parents" for our children in schools. The community, as volunteer educators, rallied to join with parents can demonstrate the extreme efforts they are willing to make on behalf of better schools and improved education. The resource is available, the catalyst must be provided. Every committed parent should immediately engage in school activities and also seek out and involve another individual to improve our schools by improving parents. Why not?

Quite convincingly, Parsons plants the seeds and tells of the heroic measures parents are capable of achieving when they know that their children are in danger. Americans must wake up and recognize that the dangers of failing to educate all of our children are real and should cause us the gravest concern. Clearly, parents must recognize the need for action and the immediacy of the challenge. For, as Cynthia Parsons says, "Groups of determined parents, joined in holy high dudgeon, can effect dramatic change in schools and schooling." Parents in very large supply must enter schools voluntarily and participate in the act of schooling our young, their future depends upon . . . improving parents.

Chapter Seven

Improving Parents

The story is told of a mother whose infant fell through an old grating covering an unused well. She tried unsuccessfully to pull the grate up, but it was padlocked onto a frame. The child, meanwhile had landed at the bottom in more than enough water to drown.

The mother, screaming for help, went through the grating, down to the bottom of the well, rescued the infant, and climbed back up to where she could continue to call out for help. The farmer who owned the field heard her, came to where she was and asked, "How'd you get in there?"

She explained, "My baby fell through so I had to get him out." He nodded his head, went for the team of horses, hitched them to the grating, and after several tries, finally pulled it out of the ground.

He remarked as he left her on the path to her home, "Amazin' what you can do if you have to."

I have a neighbor, who, when I told him that story told me about being in the horse barn when his wife called out to say that sparks from the chimney had set the roof shingles on fire. Next thing he knew he was on top of the roof with two pails, one full of water and the other half water and half grain.

But the remarkable part about it was the fact he needed a full-length ladder to get down, and could not explain how in the world he had managed to go, with a pail in each hand, from ground level to the ridge of the roof without a ladder. His main concern? His youngest son was in a crib on the second floor near the roof.

We all know similar stories of the parent who puts everything aside for the safety of his/her child.

Apparently, parents are going to have to commit a similar amount of energy and dedication if our schools aren't going to be as life-threatening to children as a drowning or fire.

We are "a nation at risk." Most curiously, we have allowed our basic free public schools to become less and less meaningful while we have erected the most compensatory superstructure to deal with what has failed us in the beginning. No other nation on earth provides what we do in community colleges, junior colleges, institutes, television courses, correspondence schools, on-campus degree programs, off-campus degree programs, schools, colleges, universities, post-graduate programs, and way after way to enter this rich world of higher education through every possible route other than the straight academic path, though that, too, is available.

Why? Why in the world did the same nation allow its free public schools to become academically hollow while it spent millions to provide ways for all who were failed by that system as children to acquire what they need as adults? Everyone has his/her answer to that question. I shall give one here; one that is, most admittedly, overly simplistic and discusses only one aspect of a very complex social phenomenon.

Parents Are Smart

Today's parents are smarter (that is, have had more schooling) than their parents. We've only really had free public schooling in all 48–50 states in the United States for four generations. But what a time-span! What an enormous knowledge explosion has taken place in those short years! What an extraordinary number of labor-saving devices have come from the industrial revolution! How the standard of living has escalated for the hourly-wage earner as well as for his boss, and his boss, and the top management, and the owners, and the consultants!

Three generations ago, more than half of all the parents

in the United States hadn't completed high school. A generation later they had. And now more than half of all parents have not only completed high school, but have gone somewhere and somehow to a post-secondary institution.

Three generations ago, parents behaved as though they were rather in awe of the local public school, its teachers and administrators. School folks talked about degrees and certificates; gave out grades and reports which parents had to sign; and when the children of those parents didn't measure up to some "school" standard, the school told the parents to come to their building and explain themselves. Parents were told what they should and should not do by school authorities. Let a parent "talk back" to a teacher, and the parent was sent to the "office."

That is, some parents were in awe of the local public schools. A good many were not. As good schools and schooling historians have written, school teaching has always been held in low esteem by the general public. First, of course, by those artisans who worked with their hands and had a beautiful product to stand behind. Later, engineers and managers could (and did) look down on those relegated to teaching children and hence left out of the American dream of using your wits to go from 30-cents-an-hour wage earner to millionaire with a big house on a hill, use of a corporate airplane, exotic travel to far-off lands, and constant exposure in the local paper's society pages.

Incidentally, here's how this low esteem works out today, Sunday after Sunday, in one newspaper, the New York Times. All wedding and engagement announcements carry background information on the bride and groom. If, and only if, either has attended a private, independent, or parochial secondary school is the school's name included. If, on the other hand, either went to a public school, the name of the school is omitted.

Even though a generation ago a good many parents knew that the "smarter" products of the local schools weren't choosing teaching as a career, nevertheless, there was a certain admiration for those who did choose teaching. And two and three generations, when more than half of all school-age children lived with both parents, one or both parents thought it was their solemn duty to support the local school as well as its teachers. They disciplined their children at home after they were punished at school; they monitored homework duties, taking them seriously and giving their children the impression they were in league with the teachers in this matter.

Parents Are Choosers

Also, and this is critical to why our schools so badly need improving in the 1980s, some parents were able to "buy" their way out of the local free public schools. It's in New England that we had the first free public school; it's also in New England that we carried from the mother country the concept that lower social class children did not (with a few rare, proven "brilliant" exceptions) attend the same schools—or receive the same schooling—as children from upper class homes.

Churches, themselves made up of congregations of selected socioeconomic stratas, held tight sway over many schools both public and private. The Roman Catholic church in the United States, through its parish system, opened its own schools in direct competition with the Protestant-dominated public schools, and parents were supposed to place the "brighter" and "more promising" of their youngsters in these parochial schools, while often placing in the local public school the "lesser" family lights.

Thousands of teachers, both in public as well as non-public schools, have made sure their children did not (and still do not) attend a local public school, but a private one—testimony to how they perceive the schools they serve.

Further, when the children three generations ago went from school to college, they moved from city to suburb. Zoning laws permitted them to create socioeconomically stratified communities. Here, the local public school aped the New England private co-educational day school. The same architects (or copiers of the same) designed buildings for these rival groups; the same textbook companies published a line of texts for these students; and while in many instances (hard to beat a New York City teacher's salary) the salary wasn't higher for these teachers, the working conditions provided some compensation, and there were always those long summers either to be used to earn income or for personal gratification.

Attendance zoning made it possible for one building in a school district to have one set of standards for teachers and equipment, while another suffered by comparison. A generation ago, when desegregation efforts were forcing disclosures and changes, it was revealed just how very badly off were those schools with a high percentage of minority and/or poor children.

It didn't take long, for example, when white sixth graders in Tampa were forced to leave their suburban-like schools to spend a year in an inner-city building, for parents to raise an enormous howl. The buildings didn't just need cleaning and painting and modern plumbing and lighting, but, the white parents argued, better teachers, secretaries, administrators, and specialists. It also didn't take long for the schools to divide into class groups on the basis of past classroom performance and test results.

This, of course, served to redivide the children into socioeconomic and racial groupings.

Yes, as parents acquired schooling, and it came time for them to send their children to school, they not only recognized how important were those basic lessons, but increasingly recognized that teaching was not the profession for those who wanted "to maximize their earning power."

Also, parents, ever wanting the "best" for their children, and operating on that grand motive of protection for their "babies," worked to be sure that local public schools were under local control. In many of the Southern states, as we all well know, this translated into programming two separate school systems, one for black children and one for white. In the rest of the states, attendance zones served to create similar ghetto schools. Almost every city in Texas is a marvel of this contrivance, and many of the larger ranches in Texas zone themselves right out of any school district at all—a considerable tax savings for the owners, forcing the children of the ranch hands to take long bus rides to get to a school.

The city of Boston, for several generations up until this last one, managed to create attendance zones and school transportation patterns, and to support a huge nonpublic school system, carefully keeping within racial housing patterns, making it no more school-system integrated than Atlanta in the 1950s.

California created its ghettos with its zoning requirements. Yet, it not only did not support a large nonpublic school movement, but early decided that every student who completed high school should go right on to college; and which institution each attended was not determined fiscally, but academically.

At the same time that California has been a "model" of access to higher education, it also has been a "model" for unfair funding of public school districts. A dramatic geographical example of this is the island known as the Beverly Hills School District, entirely surrounded by the long sea named the Los Angeles Unified School District.

Apparently parents right across our nation have wanted so very badly to give their children a head start by seeing that they got the best possible basic schooling that they have been willing to have their neighbor's child placed in a school inferior to the one their child attends.

What a cruel sentence that last one is. . . . Is it justified? Do we really want something for our children which we deny to our neighbor's? Are we really so competitive that we would draw up uneven sides to begin with? In other words, would we want our children in a race with children who didn't start at the same line?

Parents Want the Best

Ten years of common schooling; ten years when all the children of all the parents in the United States are offered the same rich school diet. Ten years to develop sound learning skills; to get started on an understanding of concepts in math and natural science. Ten years of reading and writing critical material; of doing research; of debate; of singing, dancing, painting, acting, and learning to play lifetime games.

We are the strongest democracy on earth. Being more democratic, rather than weakening us, would only strengthen us. That doesn't mean there cannot be choice, or that all schools have to be identical.

If our schools really are going to improve, then it's the parents who are going to have to be willing to help every child "make it" through those ten basic years. As Mortimer Adler proclaims: "What's best for the best is best for all."

Unless all parents want all children to have the best possible schooling in the happiest and highest quality schools, then the schools won't be able to improve radically. Yes, a few schools can adopt a few of the suggestions in this book. But no, full-scale change, in order to work in a democracy, has to be democratically arrived at.

Let me return to the question which triggered this discussion. Why . . . did the same nation allow its free public schools to become academically hollow while it spent millions to provide ways for all who were failed by that system as children to acquire what they need as adults? And the answer: because selfish parents tried to provide better schooling for their children than for all children.

In so doing, they managed to turn more and more schools over to weaker and weaker scholars until our schools are being administered by those with the lowest college-level test scores in the nation. Instead of getting what they really wanted—high quality schools—parents have created a climate for lowest-common-denominator schools.

Of course, I'm not only oversimplifying, but generalizing. There are hundreds (is it thousands?) of instances throughout the United States of parents making an enormous difference for their children and for all others. Many a strong bilingual/bicultural program, in an ethnically changing neighborhood, has flourished because it had the blessing of the majority of "old-line" parents.

Those few schools in the United States where the arts

dominate have enormous parental support and interest. And it takes extremely sensitive parents to remove the competitiveness in a public school and replace it with cooperation.

Just as those of us who travel from school to school know what kind of principal to expect because of what we learn in our walk from the parking lot to the central office, so we can quickly tell whether or not a school has the support of its parents.

You parents are the key to good schools. Without your support, few positive changes will ever take place. What do you think about this notion of children starting their formal schooling when you and the school think they are mature enough for the kindergarten program? That may be the day after your son/daughter reaches the age of four. It might be just before their fifth birthday. It might be September 1; and then again, it might happen on October 1, or April 15.

And what about young people between the ages of 16 and 26 giving two years of service to their democracy?

Considering both the maturity and naiveté of 14-year-olds, would you permit your children to alternate their time between school and a part-time job? Or, if they preferred, would you let them go to college at 14?

College at 14! It's done now, but usually by the "genius" kid; certainly not the normal pattern. What's true, though, is that scholars who know how to reach an active young academican teach, for the most part, at the college level. In fact, it's in college that the sort of scholarship an active 14-year-old craves, is available. Simon's Rock (now part of Bard) is an experiment in placing today's last two years of secondary school and the first two years of college together. Those who early supported this concept thought it would become the standard in many such institutions.

Simon's Rock

The problem is not what Bard offers, but the institutional rigidity which has so long characterized school administrators and post-secondary educationists. But that rigidity could (and should) be broken. By the time a youngster is 14, and has spent ten years in as pluralistic an academic environment as possible, it's high time that teenager moved into a community of specialists.

Suppose your youngster early showed a love of math and not only willingly spent hours on the computer playing math games, but working through basic mathematical exercises—just as other children willingly spend hours perfecting basic skills on a musical instrument; or hour upon hour reading through all the novels of Guy de Maupassant. What a travesty it would be if by the time your child is ready for independent study and research with a sound scholar, instead she/he is forced to mark time while band, cheerleading, junior proms, senior plays, yearbook sales, and varsity athletics absorb most of the waking hours.

Not every 14-year-old wants to be a serious student; but those who do need to be offered every advantage this rich nation has to offer. By the age of 14, these bright academic stars will have done yeomen duty in class after class, discussion after discussion. They will have been the leaders in learning group after learning group. And they deserve college-level thinking and college-level peers.

Those who mother these young academicians (fathers and guardians included) know what it means to keep up the level of development; and also how destructive it is to dissipate that growth with peripheral activities. We've not only consistently done this to young girls who early showed an inclination for such "male" interests as math, engineering, or physics, but we've so distracted young male scholars by demanding a social/athletic mix that they have lost the zest for study at the very time they should have been exploring ideas with all the vigor at their disposal.

Parents Seek Alternatives

Yet, for every teenager who wants to pursue academics, there is one—perhaps two—who needs to see the relevance of study before continuing. They crave some practical application and want, instead of more schooling, an opportunity to find the bottom of the job ladder and start that long climb up to job satisfaction and leadership. If we really keep our youngsters at the books for those ten years of basic schooling, then we can afford to turn the curriculum around entirely and relate learning to earning; relate classroom activity to their developing business skills. These 14-year-olds (with rare exceptions) aren't going to be of much use to most employers, except to do the unskilled and semiskilled chores around the store, factory, office, etc. What is needed is a year of work by a pair of co-op ed students (need not, of course, be the same pair of students, but the job needs full-time filling) at the unskilled level, who, for the second year on the job, would handle assignments with growing responsibility.

Of course, the main purpose of two years of co-op ed for 14-, 15-, and 16-year-olds is not so much to learn a specific work skill (filing, entering data into the computer, copying, changing tires, stacking shelves, washing windows), no, not those skills, but to learn how to be prompt, courteous, reliable, thoughtful, considerate, able to take orders, how to cooperate with all sorts of co-workers, and to be prudent, sensitive, orderly.

Spending two years working in a grocery store might teach a youngster he never wanted to have anything more to do with retailing; then again, it might have just the opposite effect. But if during two years of working in a grocery store the 14–16-year-old learned what it means to hold down a job to the satisfaction of employers and fellow employees, that is a worthy gift to all children from all the adults in this democratic nation.

And it's also very possible that the youngster who decided that getting right into a job and starting that long climb toward "maximizing earning potential" was not quite what it seemed has the option to switch into a college program. The 14-year-old can switch; or wait until the two-year co-op ed program is over, and then at 16 or 17 go to a college or university.

The Boston Fenway area is ringed with apartment houses; nearby are housing developments for low income families. Hundreds upon hundreds of children live in these homes, where little in the way of chores is available to them. Unlike the farm child, there are no chores which are regularly part of growing up. Even suburban children can be given some responsibilities toward home and community upkeep. But the millions of children spending the most formative years of their lives in dwellings with no meaning to them and not one iota of responsibility for their maintenance or beauty, and with no jobs available to them in their urban neighborhoods when they are but children, early take on habits and behaviors which stultify both working and learning abilities.

How is a boy or girl to learn thoughtfulness, promptness, cleanliness, orderliness, courtesy . . . ? How many children can we treat this way, fail to teach these qualities to, and not have them, as adults, either dependent upon us or preying upon us?

Parents Appreciate Service

Two years of compulsory national service, I'll admit, is a startling recommendation. But I believe I've sweetened it a bit by suggesting it be:

(1) taken sometime between a young adult's 16th and 26th birthdays;

(2) involved with a public service chosen by the young adult; and

(3) selected with the help of counselors in local secondary schools.

This suggestion is not a veiled method for conscription into the U.S. armed forces. I would hope, should there be sufficient interest in such a program at the highest levels of government, that literally thousands of public service jobs would be classified as suitable for these two years of national service.

And, of course, all costs for this service, including the employment of counselors in every secondary school in the nation, and reimbursement for pay to all who serve, would be a national—not a local—responsibility.

I'm sure, too, that some added incentives may have to

be included, in order that a sufficient number of young adults do choose to enter one of the branches of the military forces. Either the pay could be higher, or if the pay across all services was identical, then each person serving at a military post might earn future college credits (a form, if you will, of the GI Bill) for each year of service.

Since national service counselors, in my plan, would be in every secondary school, they could be responsible for contacting students before the age of 14 to introduce them to the range of options open to them for national service. Those students, for example, who are headed for a college or university at the age of 14 might not want to do their two years of service until they have earned a bachelor's degree.

For such a college student, his eventual choice of professional career might well dictate the type of service: for the lawyer, two years in a state attorney general's office; for the doctor, two years in a public health clinic; for the business executive, two years in a town manager's office; for the teacher, two years in a public school.

It's also possible that the college student wouldn't want to interrupt his academic course until he/she had earned a master's degree. Six years after secondary school would put that young adult at the age of 20, with six years left in which to take out two for national service. And this leaves yet another choice for the professional—interrupting a professional career with two years of service. Perhaps the young nurse or physician wonders whether he/she shouldn't have chosen law after all! Still time to spend two years in a legal-aid office, to get a close taste of what being a lawyer is all about.

By placing national service counselors in every secondary school, we would put in place an ideal flow of information for longitudinal studies.

Parents Are Monitors

Parents: You should really be annoyed at the educationists in this nation. They have not done what you have always done—they have not studied the effect their actions and decisions have made over time. Parents do this, continuously. They monitor their children day after day, month after month, year after year. They alter their parental signals on the basis of what they learn over time.

This is precisely the way educators should operate, and very very seldom do. In fact, one of the main criticisms teachers lay on their administrators is that they don't know enough about the children they are to teach; no one sees to it that they are fully briefed, and they may spend most of a school year off on a wrong tangent because of this ignorance.

And it's no secret that most high schools now operate without any follow-up data at all. They test and test and test their pupils while they are in the building, but once they leave there is no mechanism whatever for accumulating more information. Blindly the decisions are made, not on the basis of what a particular school knows about the effects of its particular program, but what a national norm has to say.

And so, with the introduction of national service, democratically administered, and with placement of national service counselors in all secondary schools, a file of raw data regarding test scores, course grades, jobs undertaken, skill evaluations, etc. would be funneled back into the originating secondary school. Access by computer linkup, would make it possible for any young adult to be served by any secondary school in the nation.

But what a marvelous way for those charged with teaching our children to follow what has happened to them in light of what they were exposed to in school.

And what a marvelous resource these national service counselors would be! To have someone in every secondary school who knows what's really happening to every single graduate is to have in place a pedagogical compass by which school administrators can better set the course(s) of study. Teachers and administrators set those courses now; and vigorously oppose many of the improvements suggested in this book, apparently out of a vast pool of ignorance. They don't know what they could have done better or differently for their former students. They don't know where their former students are or what they are doing or even what their opinion is of what they were exposed to while in school.

But let's get back to those ten basic years of schooling. There are several configurations of schools now in the United States. Generally, though, pupils spend six or seven years in an elementary school; and six years in either one high school or a two-step junior then senior high school.

If, as I suggest, we start children in school at the age of four in family-grouped classes, then we would limit each primary school to 300 pupils ages 4 to 8.

The next step, probably called a "middle" or "junior" school would house 300 children ages 8–12. It is in this middle or junior school that the classical studies would begin, but following on the primary base, the children would mix ages and interests and skills and abilities. Teaching would be more Socratic and coaching would work at the perfecting of skills.

The secondary school (or high school) would contain the children aged 12–16. Here, there could be as many as 800 youngsters, as half of those aged 14, 15, and 16 would not be in school but out on a co-op ed job, allowing the school staff to deal, at any one time, with some 500 pupils.

It is in each one of these school levels that I would house police and fire substations, health clinics, welfare offices, day care centers, wings of art museums, and the like. It is in each of these schools that I would expect to find national service personnel helping out. In each of these schools find a mix of teachers—some part-time, some full-time, some training as interns, and others serving in leadership positions as master teachers.

And it is in the secondary school that all the pupils would continue their classical education until they moved on to college or began a co-op program. It is these secondary schools which would be the most radically changed by the athletic program. Today, many a parent counts on his son or daughter participating in varsity athletics at high school preparatory to a career in athletics in college and possibly beyond.

Many high school athletic teams are "farm" teams for colleges. The high school coaches work closely with the college coaches in an old boy and new girl network which is very very tight. It will take enormous energy and dedication by parents to break this stranglehold on children's lives.

Let the athletes "do their thing," but let them do it as individuals and within a club structure. Let the athletic user pay his/her own way. And let physical education in local secondary schools meet the needs of the pupils. It's quite possible that all the businesses which hire the co-op ed students would want to sponsor their own competitive teams. All well and good, and very much within the sort of democratic structure so vital to the United States. And let our secondary schools be free to teach individual sports skills, including swimming.

Parents Are Dedicated

We're curious people, we Americans. We believe absolutely that every single person in our democracy has the same rights (and responsibilities) as every other. But we also believe something—just as absolutely—which is fairly near the opposite; that is, we believe every one of us has the right to pull ahead of our neighbor. We have the right, using our wits and energy, to get ahead of the other fellow.

It's this pair of beliefs which motivates most parents. Yes, on the one hand they want all children to have what their children want and need; and no, they don't want their children to be held back by those who aren't as XXX as their children. Sometimes XXX is "smart." Sometimes it refers to race; at times even to family wealth.

Here's how one mother went through a grate to rescue not only her child, but a whole school. Seems her daughter was chosen to play a lead part in a school play; not a big deal, but nevertheless, an important enough event so that the public would be invited to the two performances.

The daughter was concerned enough about the story line to bring a script home and talk with her mother about it. In the play she was to be sick and die; the other actors and actresses all had parts showing how this death was affecting them. The theme was morbid; a tragedy without relief.

The mother told her daughter to pull out of the play, but the daughter wept, saying she would be letting her class and teacher down. The mother called the school and made an appointment with the teacher.

By and large it was not a pleasant encounter; the teacher thought the children should learn what death and sorrow was all about and had purchased the scripts with what little discretionary money she had. She thought the mother was just being troublesome. And was most disturbed to think the best memorizer would be pulled from the cast.

Back home the mother stewed and fussed. The daughter, caught in the middle, said to her mother, "Well, why don't you write a good play for us and we'll put it on instead."

Interestingly enough, the mother had never, ever, written a script. She'd not been on stage during her school and college days; she had no courses in script writing. But she accepted the challenge. Wrote practically night and day, and when the script was completed took it to school.

Yes, it was used as a substitute; there were parts for every member of the class and not just the usual few. And the mother, you guessed it, she's been writing school plays ever since.

That's a rather extreme example of an improved parent; an extreme example of the lengths some parents may need to go to have their school do what's right, what's fair, what's of the highest possible quality; what's joyous, healthy, and healing. Yet parents are going to have to be "extreme" in many instances to jolt school officials out of their posture that almost all school problems stem from the pupils' behavior—one reason, of course, why "discipline" hits the No. 1 spot on the Gallup Poll year after year.

That's rather like the attitude displayed by a mountain-pass diner in a framed and fly-specked message which reads: "We're not so sure about our customers, but our waitresses are always right."

Or the head counselor who used to sigh, just about midnight when we'd managed to extinguish what we hoped was the last trouble spot: "What a wonderful camp this was until those darn kids arrived."

Parents Can Effect Change

If the school your child attends has a sour and mean principal, or one or more flagrantly incompetent teachers, then that's an emergency. At the very least, see to it that the superintendent and school board remove those people from direct contact with your children.

You can't easily remove them from the school, but they can be given other assignments within the school setting. There's an interesting ironical situation—a school removal treated as an emergency—which often involves parents. Many school critics spend more time and energy trying to eliminate Mark Twain's *Huck Finn* from school libraries and classrooms than they do to separate sensitive children from poor teachers.

Twain's novel doesn't talk to children, direct them, choose activities for them, read to them, judge them, evaluate and grade them, attempt to embarass them in front of their peers; Huck doesn't play favorites, or choose up sides, or offer one kind of help to one pupil and another level of concern and help to another. Good old Huck just sits on one or more shelves. Not so, incompetent teachers and administrators. They walk and talk and hurt and disturb. The pupils under their jurisdiction can't escape, unless caring parents see to it that the offending adults are removed from the teaching environment.

Huck, on the other hand, is one of the hundreds of books our children should read, and with good coaching, grow to understand. And use to get a better grasp of the flow of ideas in the world, particularly our role as democrats in this shrinking and interdependent world.

Groups of determined parents, joined together in holy

high dudgeon, can effect dramatic change in schools and schooling. There are those, who, reading that last sentence, would want to add the caveat: "For better or for worse."

I sat in on a hearing before a judge in a Phoenix, Arizona, courtroom which pitted a group of determined parents and citizens against a school district's choice of textbooks for the elementary grades. That is, they seemed a group of determined parents and citizens until one talked with the parents. They, it seemed, had been "hired" for the day, given lines to say and postures to assume, and were backdrop for a couple of "this is our cause" taxpayers.

Nevertheless, they had the school officials on the run, and had their cause had more merit, and had the parents thought the roof was really on fire, some fundamental changes would have taken place in that community's schools.

I was intimately involved when a group of parents saw to it that some members of a school board were not reelected, and a "reform" group was. A bus load of excellent teachers and administrators left the district as the direct result of one poignant election return. It took enormous efforts by another group of citizens and parents to repossess the schools.

Is this not what a democracy is all about? What a marvel our public school system is—it really does belong to the people. We have, although enormously dissipated over the past three generations, direct control of our schools. That is, we should have direct control of our schools, but we've given up much too much to unionization, collective bargaining, state department of education regulations, state tenure laws, and apathy.

Perhaps this is a good place to talk about school prayers. In the 1950s I started each teaching day in a public school by reading aloud to the class from my copy of the King James version of the Bible. Next door to me, a Roman Catholic read from the Douay Bible. And next door to him the teacher lead all the pupils in an oral recitation of her favorite version of the Lord's Prayer.

I had already started my day by praying even before I got to school. Yet, I tried not to influence my pupils, nearly all of whom over a 14-year, K–12 classroom teaching career were not members of my denomination, but held a wide variety of religious beliefs. I did as I learned many other Christians did—I read only from the Old Testament. And I tended to confine my selections to the Psalms and Proverbs.

When I became education editor of *The Christian Science Monitor* in the early '60s, the school prayer issue was heated to the boiling point. One of the editorial writers came to talk with me about the problem, definitely a tricky one for a church-owned newspaper whose members regularly pray both individually and collectively.

He started our discussion by asking if I had prayed with my pupils at the start of each school day. When I assured him that I had, he looked pleased; but I quickly followed that with my firm belief that I had been wrong; that what I had done was intrusive, and broke not only a Christian commandment but defied the Bill of Rights.

If I could, I would urge every man, woman, and child throughout the world to turn to God daily and constantly; I would urge all of us to believe in a God who is the Great Spirit that American Indians so reverence. I would ask every single one of us to start our days (as well as our nights) with prayer.

On our mental knees, we need to humble ourselves; we need to seek ways to love our fellow man enough to treat every individual as a real equal. It is a remarkable thing we do in the United States—this giving to every single child in our nation a minimum of ten years of free schooling.

May every parent start each child's day with prayer; and may every school start each child's day with courtesy and caring, helping and sharing.

Checklist Index

Checklist Index

Academics:
  for principals, 85-88, 111-112, 133
  for teachers, 53-55, 78, 81, 133
Accommodating parents, 19-20, 23-31, 34, 37, 41, 43-44, 52,
  101-105, 194-214
Administrative costs, 135, 178-193
Alternative schools, 126, 202
Art, 25-27, 85, 97-98, 113, 153, 187, 202-203
Awards, 35-36, 44, 80-81, 118, 123, 137

Beautification, 27, 42, 97, 113, 187
Be original! 104, 109-111, 176, 120-122, 125, 143-144, 153, 158,
  160, 172, 177, 181, 183, 188
Bilingual teachers, 155-157, 187, 202
Breakfast, 20, 25, 44, 125, 130
Buddy System, 20, 67, 70

Chores, 21-22, 25-26, 34-35, 43-44, 130, 178, 206
Class size, 29, 38, 62-64
Clothes box, 19, 44
Club sports, 169, 176, 182, 210
Coaching, 67, 81, 88, 93, 95, 112, 132, 137, 139, 168, 185, 209
Co-ed sports, 169, 174-175
Community school use, 24-27, 32, 34, 69, 87, 97-98, 105-106,
  108-110, 131, 157-158, 175, 178-179, 188
Compulsory swimming, 182
Computers, 152, 171, 173, 177
Conceptual teaching, 53-56, 60-61, 68-70, 94, 140-141, 143-144,
  172, 188, 201
Contracts:
  pupils, 126, 137
  teachers, 72, 80-81

Co-op ed, 27, 38-39, 97-98, 101-103, 127-130, 137, 164-170, 175, 179-180, 203, 205-206

Cooperation vs. competition, 12, 18, 20-22, 28, 30, 34-36, 44, 64, 86, 106, 116-117, 125, 137, 158, 173, 188, 203

Counselling, 25, 38-40, 44, 90, 92-93, 102, 113, 128-129, 137, 168, 176, 206

Courtesy, 32-35, 43-44, 92, 111, 117, 214

Cultural understanding, 17-19, 36-37, 42-44, 57-58, 69, 85-87, 107-109, 125-126, 136-137, 156, 162, 200, 202, 210-211

Curriculum development, 78, 103-104, 112, 176, 139-177

Dancing, 18, 25, 31-32, 43, 85, 113, 124-125, 130, 136, 153, 158, 169, 173, 180, 202

Debate, 96, 161, 175, 202

Democracy, 12, 14-17, 22, 37, 39, 41, 43-44, 99-102, 116, 126-128, 137, 149, 162-164, 170, 176, 188, 202, 205, 210, 213

Diagnostic research, 64, 75-77, 81, 90-91, 93-95, 100-101, 112, 207-209

Discipline, 17, 21, 26, 32-34, 36, 89, 113, 116-138, 148

Drama, 18, 25-26, 85, 96-97, 104, 113, 123, 137, 161, 175, 180, 202, 210-211

Driver ed, 170, 176-177

Family groupings, 20, 29-30, 103, 126, 148-149, 153, 179

Feeling (ethos/environment), 11-45, 52, 83-84, 89, 92, 103, 110-114, 119-120, 123, 212-214

Follow-up evaluation, 90, 102-103, 112-113, 187, 207-209

Field days, 158, 161, 169, 175, 181

Fiscal:
   integrity, 91-92, 189-193
   prudence, 26, 178-193

Folk music & dance, 63, 85, 173-175, 143, 154, 158, 173

Grouping & regrouping, 20,22, 29, 31, 62, 145-146, 153

Health ed, 170-171, 176-177

Helping one another, 21-22, 26-27, 29-30, 33-34, 65, 78, 103, 113, 121, 123-124, 130, 179-180

Homework, 130, 158-160, 175

"Hum," 84, 113, 124

Individualized teaching, 30-31, 34, 37-38, 40, 42, 44, 57,
    59-61, 64, 73, 75, 94-95, 107, 111, 120-123, 127, 146,
    149, 159
Integrated curriculum, 78, 173, 153-154, 175

Jury duty, 101, 113
Jury trials, 99-100, 113, 127

Language teaching, 28, 31, 69, 79, 154-156, 174, 178-179, 185
Learning styles, 55-56, 62-63, 94-95, 149-152
Libraries, 24, 77-78, 142, 145, 173, 179, 212
Lifetime sports, 158, 169, 176, 181-182, 202, 210
Listening, 26-27, 31-32, 63
Lock-step removal, 17-18, 20, 30, 104, 153, 156
Lunch, 25, 34, 69, 105, 136, 161-162, 174

Magic teachers, 119, 124, 155
Master teachers, 53, 63, 66-68, 70-72, 78-79, 81, 111-113,
    179-180, 184-186
Mentors, 25, 27-28, 32, 40, 69, 81, 85-87, 108-110, 113,
    131, 174, 183
Merit pay, 80, 91, 111-112, 134, 137, 166, 176, 183-186, 192
Music, 85-86, 113, 125, 145-146, 171, 173

National service, 14, 39-43, 98, 101-102, 113, 128-131,
    179-180, 185, 203, 206-209
Non-teaching duties, 50, 52, 90, 105, 185

Paideia proposal, 58, 81, 131-132, 164, 174, 179, 185, 201-202
Parents, 25, 27, 44-45, 58, 82, 96, 104-105, 113, 137, 159, 183,
    194-214
Part-time teachers, 27-28, 78-79, 131, 157, 180-181, 184-185, 209
Peer review, 52, 67, 80, 91, 99-101, 111-112, 185
Peer teaching:
    pupils, 21, 28-31, 34, 40, 60, 64-65, 74, 103, 121, 123, 130,
        152-153, 158, 179-180, 185
    teachers, 30, 33, 54, 59, 61, 63, 67, 69-70, 74-75, 78, 81,
        85-88, 95-96, 111
Physics, 53-57, 79, 81, 113, 161, 175, 185
Ping-Pong, 136, 162, 175

Praise, 35, 43, 153
Preschool, 25, 38, 43, 129-130, 146-148
Principals as teachers, 53-55, 63, 89-90, 104, 111, 113, 138, 185
Program budgeting, 90-91, 96, 112, 186-187, 191-193

Reading, 59, 60-62, 74-75, 81, 87, 91, 172-173, 121, 141-142,
    144-145, 153, 172-173, 179

School boards/trustees, 44, 82, 113, 137-138, 156, 181, 185,
    191, 212-213
School size, 24, 42-44, 105, 131, 178, 185-186, 209
Sex education, 171, 176-177
Sharing facilities, 24-26, 44, 105-106, 113, 131, 166, 170,
    178-179, 186, 188, 209
Singing, 25-26, 31-32, 153, 158, 169, 180
Skill practice, 32, 66-68, 73-74, 88, 159
Socratic teaching, 53, 68, 132, 168, 185, 209
Spelling, 76, 173, 94, 151-152
Starting school, 29, 43, 97, 101, 103-104, 127, 129-130,
    144-149, 157, 164, 203, 209
Student senate, 99, 103, 126-127
Superintendents, 44, 107, 113, 172, 212

Teacher:
    effectiveness, 48-82, 102-103, 113, 172, 138
    interns, 49, 71-72, 81, 111, 113, 178, 181
    reassignment, 50-51, 90, 113, 212
    retraining, 53-56, 65-70, 73, 75, 79, 81, 113, 186
Telephones, 22-23, 26, 43-44, 186
Town meeting, 98-101, 113, 118, 126
Tutoring, 27, 60, 64, 69, 85-87, 96, 121, 143, 152-153

Volunteers, 24, 26-27, 31-32, 34-35, 43, 63, 69, 85-87, 96, 103,
    108-109, 113, 131, 167, 179-183, 185

Workshops, 18, 62, 65, 111, 186
Write & rewrite, 31, 60, 65-68, 81, 88, 142-143, 173, 202